W9-BBO-092

hamburgers
& fries

AN AMERICAN STORY

ALSO BY JOHN T. EDGE

Fried Chicken: An American Story
Apple Pie: An American Story

hamburgers & fries

AN AMERICAN STORY

John T. Edge

G. P. PUTNAM'S SONS

NEW YORK

G. P. PUTNAM'S SONS
Publishers Since 1838
Published by the Penguin Group

Penguin Group (USA) Inc., 375 Hudson Street, New York, New York 10014, USA ·
Penguin Group (Canada), 10 Alcorn Avenue, Toronto, Ontario M4V 3B2, Canada
(a division of Pearson Penguin Canada Inc.) · Penguin Books Ltd, 80 Strand, London
WC2R 0RL, England · Penguin Ireland, 25 St Stephen's Green, Dublin 2, Ireland
(a division of Penguin Books Ltd) · Penguin Group (Australia), 250 Camberwell Road,
Camberwell, Victoria 3124, Australia (a division of Pearson Australia Group Pty Ltd)
· Penguin Books India Pvt Ltd, 11 Community Centre, Panchsheel Park,
New Delhi–110 017, India · Penguin Group (NZ), Cnr Airborne and Rosedale Roads,
Albany, Auckland 1310, New Zealand (a division of Pearson New Zealand Ltd)
· Penguin Books (South Africa) (Pty) Ltd, 24 Sturdee Avenue, Rosebank,
Johannesburg 2196, South Africa

Penguin Books Ltd, Registered Offices:
80 Strand, London WC2R 0RL, England

Library of Congress Cataloging-in-Publication Data

Edge, John T.
Hamburgers & fries : an American story / John T. Edge.
p. cm.
ISBN 0-399-15274-1
1. Cookery (Beef). 2. Hamburgers. 3. French fries.
I. Title: Hamburgers & fries. II. Title.
TX749.5.B43E335   2005   2005043104
394.1'2'0973—dc22

Printed in the United States of America
1   3   5   7   9   10   8   6   4   2

The book is printed on acid-free paper. ∞

Photographs © 2005 Amy Evans
Book design by Stephanie Huntwork

While the author has made every effort to provide accurate telephone numbers and Internet addresses at the time of publication, neither the publisher nor the author assumes any responsibility for errors, or for changes that occur after publication. Further, the publisher does not have any control over and does not assume any responsibility for author or third-party websites or their content.

The recipes contained in this book are to be followed exactly as written. The publisher is not responsible for your specific health or allergy needs that may require medical supervision. The publisher is not responsible for any adverse reactions to the recipes contained in this book.

FOR THE GRILL COOKS WHO WALK
THE SALTED DUCKBOARDS

You can find your way across this country using burger joints the way a navigator uses stars. . . .

—CHARLES KURALT, *CBS Sunday Morning*

Contents

Series Introduction

This is the third in a series of books that celebrates America's iconic foods. Fried chicken led off. Apple pie came next. Now hamburgers and fries. Donuts will follow. To my mind, these are small "d" democratic foods that conjure our collective childhood and call to mind the question once posed by a Chinese philosopher: "What is patriotism, but nostalgia for the foods of our youth?"

I chose these foods because they transcend interregional variation and internecine debate over origins. Recognized from the Atlantic to the Pacific as uniquely American, they evoke the culinary and cultural fabric of our nation.

Though the places profiled and the recipes detailed are keys to eating well here in the States, my intent is not to compile a list of the top purveyors. Instead, in this book and the others that accompany it, I strive to sketch the historical and cultural landscape by way of what we eat. My goal is to render our gastronomic grail.

The 21st-Century
Burger

We are, at this very moment, in the midst of a burger renaissance. Call it a season of culinary nationalism. Call it a return to comfort food in a day when comfort is harder to find. Or try my favorite: Call it a manifestation of our bipolar responses to Eric Schlosser's book and Daniel Boulud's burger.

The first six months of 2001 were epochal: In January, Houghton Mifflin published *Fast Food Nation*, Schlosser's dark deconstruction of America's love affair with buck-a-pop, mass-produced burgers. By way of statistics and polemics, Schlosser declared the corporations who peddle beef-and-bun-and-fries combos to be culpable for a unique American malaise. If sales are any indication, the book made a profound impact upon the American psyche.

Much wringing of hands and forswearing of trans fats followed. But accounts of the death of the burger were greatly ex-
aggerated. In June of that same year, Daniel Boulud, a New York
restaurateur of French birth, added the $29 db Bistro burger
to his menu. It began with ground sirloin and chuck, but ben-
efited from a stuffing of braised short ribs, preserved black
truffles, a hunk of foie gras, and a mirepoix of root vegetables.

By July, critics were posting scores and post-game analysis.
Most correspondents believed Boulud's creation to be a doff
of the toque to American excess. But there were culinary
nationalists who saw his use of foie gras and truffles as pre-
dictably Gallic. Amateur psychologists said that it was a stab at
revivifying the Schlosser-indicted burger and, by extension, the
American psyche. The Wall Street crowd, on the other hand,
read Boulud's burger as a sign from on high, a pronounce-
ment of Greenspanian proportions, a thumb-of-the-nose to
dire economic forecasts.

Everyone should have held their breath and stayed their
pens. More luxe burgers were on the way. More opportunities
awaited for those inclined to eat their way to an understanding of American identity.

Following in Boulud's wake, the Old Homestead, reputedly
the oldest steakhouse in Manhattan, introduced a $41 burger.
They staked their claim on beef from Wagyu cattle, the beer-
fed and sake-bathed prides of Japanese animal husbandry.
And the wave had not yet crested. By the summer of 2002,
Claude Troisgros of Blue Door in Miami Beach ditched the
ground beef altogether, dishing nuggets of foie gras, painted
with house-made ketchup, perched on earnest brioche.

Out west, RNM, a San Francisco boîte frequented by the terminally hip, began serving Lilliputian burgers draped in white cheddar on matchbox-sized focaccia buns. And the boys at Chat Noir in Costa Mesa, California, decided to grind their Kobe beef to order and plop a lobe of foie gras right on top, where everyone could see it. Just up the coast, at Father's Office in Santa Monica, chef Sang Yoon exhibited comparative restraint, serving up a burger embellished with a comparatively homespun compote of onions and bacon.

In Minneapolis, the au courant Vincent restaurant began stuffing their burgers with short ribs and smoked Gouda. Back in New York, Pierre Schaedelin of Le Cirque 2000 pledged his devotion to the church of White Castle by way of burgers goosed with caramelized onions and sautéed porcini mushrooms.

During the winter of 2003, Richard Blais of Atlanta debuted his theater of the absurd act. As a veteran of El Bulli, Ferran Adria's surrealist Spanish restaurant, he knew a few things about the intersection of Dada and dinner. At a tony restaurant in Atlanta, he peddled tissue-wrapped Cristal burgers (a riff on the locally famous sliders served by the Krystal chain, not to mention a concurrent nod to Cristal champagne). And in a stroke of genius, he kicked the fries in favor of a foie gras milkshake chaser.

Boulud did not dither. He added freshly shaved truffles to his burger, dubbed the result a Royale, and hiked his price to $59. And still they nipped at his heels.

Rumors circulated of a Cincinnati restaurateur who gilded burger buns with 23-karat gold leaf. And then there was the seemingly apocryphal story of the overzealous Napa Valley chef who planned to raise, slaughter, and grind his own beef; harvest and thresh the wheat for his buns; and pull the teats of the heifer whose milk would become cheddar. But word has it that burger never emerged from beta testing.

In the spring of 2004, Boulud fired back. His response was uncharacteristically blunt. Boulud just piled on more truffles and jacked the price. To $99. Of course, that tariff included a quiver of soufflé potatoes, served in a silver chalice with a crock of Madeira-and-horseradish-infused aïoli.

The inevitable correction came in the summer of 2004. Ferran Adria, culinary sire of Richard Blais, announced the debut of his own burger joint, Fast Good, across the Atlantic in Madrid. He promised burgers made from sustainably raised Galician beef and fries cooked in extra-virgin olive oil. But he was quick to admit that the American burger and fries paradigm was not easy to master. "We spent eight months on the French fries," he told a reporter. "We were about ready to kill ourselves."

At about that same time, New York restaurateur Danny Meyer fired what may prove to be the fatal shot across the flattop. His new Shake Shack, a retro walk-up in Madison Square Park, eschewed all folderol and claimed greatness based upon burgers built from nothing but ground sirloin and brisket. American cheese was, of course, extra.

By the time you read these words, we may have truly come to our senses; we may be back to eating our burgers with

Heinz and French's. And on those occasions when we choose to dine opulently, our foie gras will arrive the way Escoffier would have wanted it, in a puddle of something sweet and sticky, alongside a glass of Sauternes.

t he Schlosser-Boulud seesaw of public opinion and palate plays out in the pages that follow. In both historical context and present-day practice, the polarities reflect our conflicting drives as Americans: frugal and excessive; egalitarian and exclusive; aspirational and practical; heterogeneous and homogeneous.

Burgers and fries embody those impulses. They are responses to local prejudices; they are homages to local patrimony. All are of long note or have, through swift and widespread adoption, proved to be ingrained totems of local taste. All are vernacular. All are honest. All are unabashedly American.

The Original
Expense-Account Burger

The roots of the gourmet burger phenomenon are historical. I'm talking eons. Back before the 1980s when California wunderkind Jeremiah Tower began showering his burgers with shaved black truffles from the Périgord. Not long after Manhattan's 21 Club figured out that a handful of minced celery was just what a half pound of ground sirloin required. Though the 21 Club has since reformulated its burger, ditching the celery and adding duck fat to the grind, here's my take on the recipe that made them famous.

- 2 tablespoons vegetable oil
- ¼ cup cooked celery, chopped fine
- 2 pounds ground sirloin
- ¼ cup bread crumbs
- ¼ teaspoon nutmeg
- Dash Worcestershire sauce
- Salt and pepper, to taste

- Garnishes and condiments
- 6 buns

Preheat the oven to 350°. In a small skillet, heat 1 tablespoon of vegetable oil over medium-high heat. Sauté the celery until it is just a little soft and slightly translucent. Remove from heat and allow to cool slightly. In a mixing bowl, combine all of the ingredients (except, of course, the condiments and buns) by hand, using rapid motions, without overworking the mixture. Shape into 6 round patties. Heat a little vegetable oil in an ovenproof skillet.

When the pan is very hot, cook the patties quickly (about 2 minutes) on one side. Flip the burgers and immediately put the skillet in the oven and cook the meat until done to taste (about 5 minutes for medium-rare). Place the patties on buns, along with your favorite garnishes and condiments. *Serves 6*

the
early
years

ONE

Mongols on the Move

g oogle hamburger history, and you'll soon be reading of thirteenth-century warlord Genghis Khan and his fierce cavalry. According to prevailing Internet wisdom (not to mention a goodly number of books), the Mongol leader of the Golden Horde did more than merely conquer vast swathes of the globe. Indeed, the emperor of all emperors invented the hamburger.

Here's how the story is told: The Mongols were horsemen who rarely left their mounts. Since the army required food that could be eaten while galloping, between plunders and pillages, they stored raw mutton scraps in the gap between the horse's flank and the saddle. (Think primal trail mix and you're halfway home.)

After a morning of traversing, say, the arid steppes, tough meat emerged tenderized. All a hungry warrior need do was reach beneath his saddle, scoop out a patty of meat, and chomp away.

Returning to the Internet to probe deeper, you might read of Genghis's grandson, Kublai Khan, who invaded Moscow in 1238, bringing with him a taste for pounded meat. Of course, the Russians also recognized the superiority of this technique and soon adapted it for their own purposes, garnishing chopped raw mutton (and later beef) with onion and egg and dubbing the dish steak Tartar—Tartar being their name for the Mongols.

Somewhere along the way, say, in the sixteenth century, ships from Hamburg, the most important German port of the day, began to cross the Baltic Sea with regularity, docking at Russian ports where minced beef dishes were popular. And soon German seamen returned home with a taste for minced raw beef. But their wives, inured to the foul habits seamen pick up while away from home, refused to serve such barbaric fare. Instead, the Hamburg fraus began frying and broiling those patties.

Turns out the women of Hamburg were quite good at it, so good that seafaring men of many a nation came to know a cooked patty of minced beef as a Hamburg steak. Sure, it would take a few centuries and a transoceanic leap before the steak met bun—not to mention fries and ketchup—but there you have it: the basic story, in all its facile glory, of how the Mongol horde begat the Big Mac.

———

this tale is flawed. The history of proletarian dishes like hamburgers is rarely explained by a linear progression of events. Mongols did not invent chopped meat—such dishes were popular back in the days of the Roman Empire. In fact, as Los Angeles burger hound Charles Perry has pointed out, a second-century Roman cookbook features an entire chapter of chopped meat dishes. And yet there is much to ponder in the telling of the tale, much that is uniquely American.

Take those Mongols. Substitute ten-gallon Stetsons for their traditional fur-trimmed skull caps, take into account dependence upon equine locomotion, and soon they begin to resemble the chap-clad cowboys who ranged America's frontiers. Perhaps one of the reasons so many Americans have latched onto this story is that, in the telling, we recognize a bit of our own myth-making. Take into account the Mongols' need to eat while riding, and you see a glimmer of the peripatetic Americans whose wanderlust would reach fullest flower in the 1950s, when the automobile became the darling of the working class and hamburgers proved to be ideal on-the-go sustenance.

the true story of the hamburger's origins is more prosaic. Of course Hamburg, Germany, plays a role. But the real action takes place in America, where Hamburg steaks beget hamburg steaks, hamburgs, hamburgers, and, finally—by

means of the cumulative effects of distillatory coinage—
burgers.

the writings of epicurean Louis Szathmary reveal that, by
the late 1700s, sausages of minced and seasoned beef were
known to the British as Hamburg sausages. By as early as 1834,
the menu of Delmonico's in New York City advertised a Hamburger steak. The circa 1850 popularization of the commercially produced meat grinder provided further propulsion.

Newspaper morgues yielded more clues. An 1889 edition
of the *Walla Walla Union* of Washington State describes a hash
house where patrons learned their choices from a barker who
chanted "porkchopsbeefsteakhamandeggshamburgsteakor-
liver." In addition to confirming that Hamburg steak had, by
the late 1800s, become part of the American vernacular, the
Walla Walla reference illustrates that the proto-burger had
achieved bicoastal status.

A 1900 article in the *New York Sun* reveals, interestingly, that
the term "Hamburg steak" did not resonate back in Germany:

> "When in Hamburg, we supposed we must do as the Ham-
> burgers did," reported a European correspondent. "[S]o at
> our first meal, we asked for Hamburg steak. Besides, we
> wanted to see how that viand would taste upon its native
> heath. . . . But to all our requests, couched in our best scholas-
> tic German, the waiter shook his head. Like many another
> prophet, the Hamburg steak was apparently without honor
> in its own country. . . . 'Oh well,' we said, 'just bring us an or-

dinary beef steak.' But lo and behold, when the meat was
served, there it was all chopped up and made into small
cakes—what Americans call in fact, 'Hamburg steak!'"

To a resident of Hamburg, Germany, at the cusp of the
twentieth century, fried cakes of minced beef and chopped
onions, bound with a bit of egg or bread crumbs, were steaks.
Not Hamburg steaks. Not steaks cooked in the Hamburg
style. Just steaks. No further explanation is needed. That's
how it's done around Hamburg. Only in a foreign land like
America is the modifier Hamburg required to make an
eater's preferences known.

given my druthers, I would sit down with Louis Szathmary and talk through the research he compiled on his
adopted homeland. But he passed away back in 1996. As it is,
I feel lucky that a friend sent along a few of his unpublished
musings on burgers, a veritable mother lode. And I'm thinking they may hold the key to divining a theory of burger evolution. So I return my attention to the late gastronome.
Here's what I learn:

Szathmary was a slab of a man, with quick, glinting eyes
and a Fu Manchu mustache. In every picture I've seen,
he appears resplendent in a white chef's coat and a pleated
toque. Born in Budapest, Hungary, in 1919, he received a
master's in journalism and a doctorate in psychology before

sailing into New York harbor in 1951 aboard the S.S. *Hershey*. He arrived with one dollar and ten cents to his name. And he arrived hungry.

Szathmary's brother, Geza, met him at the gangplank and directed Louis to a nearby burger stand. There, he tasted a burger topped with "ketchup, mustard, chopped onions, piccalilli, French fries, a slice of tomato, a piece of wilted lettuce," all tucked inside a bun that "vaguely resembled an Austrian Kaiser roll, but was slightly sweet, had a soft texture on the outside, and a thin crunchy surface from the griddle." From that first bite, Louis Szathmary was hooked. "That hamburger was pure heaven," he recalled. "I will remember its taste forever."

To finance future burgers, Szathmary followed an immigrant's path: He took a restaurant job. At the time, he saw it as a stopgap measure. But his wartime training in Hungarian army canteens proved to be a more easily marketed skill than psychology. Within four years, he was executive chef of the Mutual Broadcasting System, the largest network of radio stations in the nation. In succeeding decades, he worked as a culinary consultant, developing, among other foodstuffs, frozen dinners for Stouffer's. By the early 1960s, he operated his own Chicago restaurant, The Bakery.

When Szathmary wasn't cooking, he was collecting books and culinary ephemera. Along the way, he got his hands on a handwritten grocery list penned by John Hancock; a menu from Abraham Lincoln's 1865 inaugural banquet; and a letter from a neighbor to Ben Franklin, asking Betsy Franklin for advice on ridding salt pork of maggots. Szathmary realized the value of such items at a time when few others did.

And God bless him, Szathmary realized the import of hamburger lore and idiom, the promise of which led me to Johnson & Wales University in Providence, Rhode Island, where, until recently, Szathmary's daughter, Barbara Kuck, managed his culinary collection. When I call Barbara to make arrangements, she says in not so many words, "What took you so long?"

With Kuck at my side, I spend a day rooting through a box of burger research that Szathmary intended to fashion into a book. Among the treasures lurking within is his survey of charitable cookbooks, spanning the years 1900 through 1990. A few salient discoveries:

Szathmary consulted 3,232 ground beef recipes in 1,108 cookbooks and found that, in the first decade of the twentieth century, the term "hamburger" was used eleven times in a recipe title. (That's earlier and perhaps more frequently than prevailing citations.) What's more, he divined that, by the 1930s, cooks were already playing fast and loose with burgers, adding, among other things, brown sugar and chopped gherkins to the mix. In other words, when most people would place the burger at the brink of canonization, Szathmary was documenting its evolution.

But what really makes my heart go pitter-patter is a book I find at the back of the box, *Hamburger for America and the World: A Handbook of the Transworld Hamburger Culture*. It's a 133-page monograph, written by Gyula Décsy of Bloomington, Indiana, and published in 1984 as part of a series that examined "national identity from the point of view of global anthropology."

In addition to an 808-entry accounting of Décsy's Hamburgensia Collection—everything from a 1976 vintage box of Gaines Burgers dog food, to a 1984 *Good Morning America* transcript reference to a Chinese burger corporation then operating in the U.S.—it includes an introduction by Szathmary.

The big man makes some interesting points, among them that Americans glommed on to hamburgers because, during our nation's formative years, we were largely a bachelor workforce, lacking female companions and cooks. Women have historically braised meat, he points out; they tend to cook roasts slowly in simmering liquid. Men typically cook meats with dry heat, by broiling and grilling and griddling. And so, according to Szathmary, in male-dominated America, dry-cooked burgers came to the fore.

In succeeding paragraphs, Szathmary also argues that men embraced burgers because buns reminded them of the maternal bosom. And he posits that the very name hamburg(er) conjured a randy seaport with "the most notorious nightlife establishments of the continental shoreline." But his theories of gender and ground beef do greatest service to our cause of understanding when he turns his attention to a reading of immigration.

"When the immigrants came from the Germanic, Scandinavian, and other northern parts of Europe," Szathmary wrote, "the main port of embarkation for the New World used to be Hamburg. This was the last city in Europe, regardless of where the emigrant came from. He could be a Czech from Prague, a Bavarian from Munich, a Saxon from Leipzig, a Prussian from Berlin, a Pole from Warsaw—the last piece of European soil he felt under his feet was the soil of Hamburg. This was the place of farewell from the Old World, from family, from mother, sister, wife, daughter, sweetheart; in other words, from any and every female companionship."

Décsy also assumes this line of thought in his opening remarks. He, too, believes the act of immigration is key, though he doesn't embrace Szathmary's gender theories. Décsy imagines the many ethnic groups who booked passage for America from the port of Hamburg. He enumerates the names each ascribe to their favorite ground meat dishes, the *frikadelle* of Northern Germany and the *faschiert* of Germanic Austria, the Slovak *fašírka,* the Polish *farsz,* the Hungarian *fašírozott.* And then he asks you to hear these men aboard the boats of the Hamburg-German Line, bantering back and forth, concocting a pidgin dialect of their own, a dialect wherein Hamburg steak comes to mean *patty of ground meat* to many people.

By this point, steak cooked in the manner of Hamburg has lost its moorings. It's no longer appropriate to identify it as a product of Hamburg, Germany. Instead it becomes a culinary lingua franca for all manner of griddled and broiled meat patties. Of course, natives of central Europe may believe that something of import was lost in translation.

And they're probably right; but it could be worse. Consider, for example, that all-American treat, Vienna sausages. Something tells me that the sons and daughters of Vienna, Austria, would never deign to recognize their beloved wursts in our tinned nubs of emulsified chicken and pork, bound by corn syrup and hydrolyzed soy protein, and brightened by a soupçon of sodium nitrate.

Hanna's 19th-Century Hamburger

The earlier reference to Hamburg sausages was from The Art of Cookery Made Plain and Easy, *written by Englishwoman Hanna Glasse, and originally published in 1747. Szathmary likely looked to the 1803 revision, published in Virginia, for inspiration when, in 1986, he developed this modern interpretation. Szathmary suggests serving the patties on "lightly toasted English muffin[s] with mustard and a slice of onion, but no lettuce and tomato."*

- 1¾ pounds beef chuck, cut into half-inch cubes, with half run *once* through a grinder set to large holes, and half run twice through. (Keep halves separate.)
- 1 teaspoon salt
- ½ teaspoon coarsely ground black pepper
- Pinch of ground cloves
- Pinch of mace
- ½ teaspoon dried marjoram leaf, crushed fine between your palms
- 2 large eggs, beaten

- 8 English muffins
- 1 onion, sliced
- Mustard

If the butcher hasn't ground your meat, proceed with the grinding instructions as specified in the ingredient list. Place in a bowl, cover, and refrigerate. Set aside the once-ground meat. To the twice-ground meat, add salt, pepper, cloves, mace, marjoram, and eggs, working together with your hands until the mixture is well combined, almost smooth in texture. Let the mixture stand, covered, on your counter, for 1 hour. Then refrigerate for at least 5 hours (or overnight).

Gently combine the two meats, working to distribute the egg-rich beef into the once-ground beef. Form into 8 patties and place in the freezer for 15 minutes. Remove and pan-fry for 2 minutes per side or until the patty juices run clear when pierced.

Serve, as Szathmary would have it, topped with onion on mustard-smeared English muffins. *Serves 8*
Please note that the mixture must stand and then chill 6 hours before cooking. You may want to ask the butcher to grind the meat for you according to the preceding directions, or you can do it at home.

To Hell with History!

i t is customary among chroniclers of hamburger lore to
shine a bright light on the moment when burger finally
met bun. For the most part, the telling of such tales is an exercise in fiction, for none of these accounts is truly verifiable.
(Each is, however, commemorated by a proclamation of pri-
macy from its respective state legislature.)

Most stories focus upon a festival of some sort. One oft-
quoted tale is of the Outagamie County Fair of 1885, staged
in Seymour, Wisconsin, where fifteen-year-old Charlie Na-
green supposedly slipped a butter-broiled meatball between
two slices of bread and dubbed the innovation a hamburger.
Another is of the Erie County Fair of that same year, held in
Hamburg, New York, where the brothers Menches of Canton,
Ohio, allegedly ran out of ground pork for their famous
sandwiches and resorted to ground beef.

Or perhaps the marriage of beef and bun occurred at a
Fourth of July party, held on the farm of Oscar Bilby, near the
town of Sapulpa, Oklahoma. (At Weber's Drive-In of nearby
Tulsa, Bilby's great-grandson cooks on a griddle incised with
an 1891 date as well as his forebear's initials.)

And then there's the story of Fletcher Davis of Athens,
Texas, whom natives of the Lone Star State tout as the man
who introduced burgers to the masses at the St. Louis World's
Fair of 1904.

Contrary to these festival theses, the Lassen family of Connecticut claims that family patriarch Louis Lassen cooked the

first burger in 1900 on a vertical broiler, one of the very same broilers still in service today at Louis' Lunch in New Haven.

But man cannot live on abstraction alone, and right now, I've grown weary of historical speculation. I just want a burger. I want to hear the low hiss of a patty hitting a flattop. I want to smell the caramel sweetness of onions frying. I want to scald my tongue on a goldenrod slice of American cheese as it trails down the craggy circumference of that patty. Fortunately, I know just where to find that burger: El Reno, Oklahoma.

Hard Time Onions

i sit in a rental car, idling in front of the Cheeretts Studio, where the adolescents of El Reno, Oklahoma, receive instruction in pom-pom shaking and baton twirling. I'm comfortable in my subcompact cocoon; I've got the air conditioner set to stun, and the Merle Haggard song "Okie from Muscogee" is playing on the radio.

My cell phone rings. Otis Bruce is on the line, returning my call. I tell him that I just ate an onion burger next door at Johnnie's Grill, where my countermates recommended an interview with him. They said he knew the history of El Reno's burger joints and their near universal habit of smashing onion rounds into ground beef patties as they sizzle. "Did I call the right man?" I ask. "Are you the former owner of Johnnie's?"

A long silence follows, one of those pregnant pauses during

which you know the person on the other end of the line is calculating whether they can disconnect and hope you'll chalk it up to a ghost in the machine. But Bruce bites. He tells me that he started at Johnnie's in 1956 when he was just a lad. He tells me the requisite story of how cheap those burgers were. (Seven for a buck.) And then he tells me that the onion burgers of El Reno, Oklahoma, are really New York imports.

Bruce says: "I've always heard that we got the idea of smashing onions into burgers from the New York World's Fair." I seek common ground, agreeing that, yes, the marriage of onions and ground beef has a long history and has been widely adopted. But I'm a little disappointed, as my research suggested that onion burgers are of local origin.

Sure, I've only been in town a couple hours. But I *have* been to the local library, where I engaged the head of the reference department in what I recall as a well-informed interrogation. And I have read the required onion burger literature, including an article in *Gourmet,* a disquisition in *Oklahoma Highways,* and the full run of *This and That,* Butch Bridge's Oklahoma history newsletter.

Bent on making sense of the local onion burger cult, I make the rounds of El Reno's other burger joints: Jobe's Drive-In, Robert's Grill, and Sid's Diner. And between bites I ask everyone who will meet my gaze why, at least locally, a burger isn't a burger unless it's raggedy with caramelized onions, smashed into the patty until chuck and onion are one.

El Reno folks tell me this: onions add flavor. Of course they're right, but the tradition is too ingrained—and too peculiar—to be explained away in such a fashion. In the telling, I hear something that reminds me of the late 1970s, when merchandisers of Lipton Cup-A-Soup managed to convince half of America that hamburgers weren't hamburgers unless the meat was spiked with packets of their oniony sawdust. (The result, I hasten to add, was not worthy of comparison to an El Reno onion burger.)

I am paying my tab at Sid's, plotting a drive south to Ardmore, where the Hamburger Inn has been peddling onion burgers since 1938, when I fall into conversation with Marty Hall, proprietor of Sid's. I ask my questions of him. And instead of talking about the aromatic qualities of allium, he takes me by the arm, steers me out the front door, and points to a storefront on Route 66. According to Marty, that's where a man named Ross Davis ran an eight-stool burger joint called the Hamburger Inn.

"He got it started," says Hall. "It was back in the twenties, back during the Depression. Onions were cheap then and hamburger meat was expensive. Same as it is now. But we were a lot poorer then. So Ross came up with this idea of adding onions to the burgers and smashing them into the meat with the back of his spatula. He called them Depression burgers and he'd smash a half-onion's worth of shreds into a five-cent burger. His way, the burger looked bigger. And then he'd reach for an old coffee can at the edge of the griddle and pour on a little bacon grease from breakfast. He always told me, 'You can't cook an onion without grease.'

"From there, it just spread," Marty continues. "At that time, Ross's place was at the intersection of the east-west road—Route 66—and the north-south road—Highway 81. He had people up and down the highway talking 'bout his onion burgers, imitating what he was doing. Now I'm doing the same thing, just imitating what Russ started."

I like Marty Hall. He does more than sling hash. He's an unofficial town historian, who decoupages his counter-tops with the class portraits of long-closed El Reno grade schools. And I like his burger, which, compared with the other local offerings, has a looser texture, embedded within which is a snarl of onions that shades toward black rather than brown. Most of all, I appreciate Hall's confirmation of my own theory. Sure, the onion burger is basic enough that it likely surfaced in many places at about the same time. I'd just like to think that El Reno is one of them. As far as I'm con-cerned, anyone who cares enough to wonder aloud about the same matters is a kindred spirit.

The onions were, in the lexicon of a gambler, the tell. Their presence bespoke a frugal impulse that is more univer-sal than local. Like other iconic American dishes, the taste for burgers laced with onions was wrought during days of priva-tion. Eventually, acquired taste spurred localized tradition.

What's more, their aroma called to mind my recent library research on archaic hamburger recipes. Paging through the *Bohemian-American Cookbook* of 1915, I came upon a recipe that instructed cooks making *hambursky steak* to mix one onion into every two pounds of ground beef. More explicitly, the *Boston Cooking School Cookbook* of 1883 called for hammering two to three onions into each pound of round steak. Many early recipes for hamburger and hamburger steak marry beef and onion.

Cookbooks may advance Hall's onion as sociohistorical marker theory, but my time spent at burger joints drives it home. I'm thinking of, among many others spots, the Cozy Inn of Salina, Kansas, where, since 1922, they've cooked nickel-thin burgers on a griddle stacked with sliced onions; Ferrell's Snappy Service in Hopkinsville, Kentucky, frying onions and burgers since 1936; White Mana, the monochromatic pride of Hackensack, New Jersey; and Lee's Hamburgers of New Orleans, where they know burgers absent onions by the derisive name of scrapes, as in a burger from which the good stuff has been scraped. And, of course, I'm thinking of White Castle, the 1921 vintage überchain where, after a long flirtation, ground beef patties and minced onion were wed.

Perhaps a burger heaped with onions might be best understood as a vestige of the dish's formative years, when ketchup was sometimes made from walnuts or mushrooms, and fries were still mostly the province of French and Belgian cooks. But most likely it's a vestige of an era when the fiscal bellwether dipped and burger economics followed. When I eat an onion burger today, I taste a dish that harkens to a time when men like Ross Davis hewed a tradition from the flint of poverty.

Onion-Entangled Griddle Burgers

This is the recipe that surprises everyone. It's too simple to be good, they say. It's too straightforward. And then they taste it. And they're soon fellow acolytes of the onion burger church. While working on this book, I turned most often to this recipe. More than any other way with a burger, it fueled my writings and ruminations.

- 1 pound ground chuck (beef shoulder)
- 2 onions, shaved *(use a mandolin or a very sharp knife to make the thinnest possible slices)*
- 1 teaspoon salt
- 6 slices American cheese

- 6 buns
- Mustard

Heat a heavy, well-oiled skillet over medium-high heat for 5 minutes. Loosely gather a handful of meat and slip it into the pan. Repeat a total of 6 times, working in batches as needed. The burgers should be free-form lumps.

(continued)

With the side of a spatula, push the burgers into a semblance of a round. After about a minute, pile on all the onions, add half the salt, and then, with as much force as you can manage, smash the onions into the meat. Again, work the sides of the patties into a round. Cook another minute and then flip. Smash the burgers again, hard.

Drain some of the grease that collects. Sprinkle on the remaining salt. Arrange the cheese on top and cook until the cheese melts and you smell the onions starting to burn.

Serve on mustard-garnished buns. *Serves 6*

Ours Alone

Compared to fried chicken, apple pie, and donuts—the other foods that constitute this series—hamburgers are American by birth as well as adaptation. The Dutch likely bequeathed the donut. England has a long and proud tradition of apple pie cookery. Everyone from the Viennese to the Chinese can claim fried chicken as their own. But burgers are unique. They are ours alone.

The burgers of northeastern Mississippi are especially evocative of the early days. As with the addition of onions, recipes for bread burgers and dough burgers and slug burgers served thereabouts may have been the fruit of poverty. But as I explain in the chapter that follows, many of our long-held traditions have ossified. They now thrive in less lean times.

THREE

On the Slug Trail

i n the fall of 1983, or maybe it was the summer of 1984, Willie Weeks, proprietor of Weeks Café in Booneville, Mississippi, and scion of a local burger dynasty, accepted a consulting job with a restaurant being built seventy-five or so miles southwest of Booneville in my hometown of Oxford.

The specialty of the house at Box Head's Burgers was a kind of hamburger, iterations of which are known to natives of Tippah, Alcorn, Tishomingo, Union, and Prentiss counties in northeastern Mississippi as tater burgers, cracker burgers, dough burgers, and slug burgers.

Despite the benefit of Weeks's counsel, the new café opened and closed in about six months. "Box Head's had image issues," Weeks told me. "People in Oxford didn't understand old-fashioned hamburgers. It just didn't translate."

the roots of the translation problem are historical. Old-fashioned hamburgers of the kind Box Head's once sold—and Willie Weeks still sells—are, more than likely, vestiges of the early years, codified during World War I. In an effort to ensure that soldiers fighting in the European theater received their recommended daily allowance of red meat, various federal agencies encouraged homemakers and restaurateurs to serve one meatless meal a day and to make burgers, meatballs, and meatloaves with all manner of extenders including potato meal, cornmeal, and cracker meal.

The Great Depression sparked another season of frugality. And with it came a surge in the popularity of ground meat mixes bound with eggs or a paste of flour and water. By the time the Japanese bombed Pearl Harbor, what began as an ad hoc response to meat shortages and situational poverty became formalized by way of commercially produced ground beef substitutes. They had snappy names like Numete, made from peanuts and corn flour, and Proteena, a concoction of soybean meal, tomato juice, and yeast extract.

The story of America's affair with aberrant burgers should have ended on V-J day or soon thereafter when government rationing of beef ceased. But somehow, in a number of isolated communities, especially in the deepest South—in what was for the longest time the poverty-riddled South—a taste for burgers cut with fillers has endured. That tradition remains strongest in and around two Mississippi courthouse-square towns: Booneville in Prentiss County, and Corinth in

Alcorn County. Hereabouts, more than twenty spots serve soy meal–stoked slug burgers, flour and water–cut dough burgers, and a host of other variations.

i visit Booneville first. At Joe's Burger Shop, a particleboard-paneled diner catercorner from the old rail depot, I bite into a bun stuffed with a thick round of onion, two or three shredded dill pickles, a smear of mustard, and what looks like an egg foo yong patty but tastes like a slurried beef pancake. Behind the counter stands Anita Rowland, a tall brunette. Along with her husband, Joe, she sells dough burgers for a buck a pop.

Though Rowland is happy to entertain my questions about the origins and precepts of dough burgers, she acknowledges that she is a bit shaky when it comes to names and dates. For the level of detail I require, Anita recommends an audience with the Booneville graybeards, a band of retired farmers who hold court in a domino parlor set in a derelict building in the shadow of the courthouse. "They might know more than I do," she says, "and promise me that if you find out something good you'll come back and tell it to me."

It's ten in the morning when I pay my tab and exit. My Booneville tour is less than two hours old, and yet even before my visit with Anita, I had found the time to sample a slug burger from Nell's on State Street and a dough burger from Danny's Italian Beef on Church Street. I arrived secure in the belief that I understood the local burger, but I have, with each one I've eaten, with each change in nomenclature, ingredients, and technique, grown more and more confused.

I find the domino players where Anita promised I would, in an abandoned storefront two doors down from a Jehovah's Witness meeting hall. The men sit hunched over a card table by the front window, slapping tiles onto the vinyl and cursing absently. Over the course of a half hour of leaning against the door frame and asking earnest questions, I learn that, though the Weeks family claims a burger lineage that dates back as early as 1917—and though they are widely recognized as progenitors of the prevailing burger tradition—the Weekses are thought to be a bit out of step with local custom. "Dough burgers are what we eat here," says a jowly man of fifty or so. "Willie serves a *slug* burger," he says of his neighbor, whose café is just four blocks away. "That's different. And you know, his people aren't from here; they're from up at Corinth."

When I attempt to clarify the difference between a slug burger and a dough burger, he ignores my query twice before screwing his face into a scowl and suggesting that I should ask the ladies at the library such vexing questions of local history. In an effort to keep the peace, I choose not to ask how the mere nineteen miles between Corinth and Booneville begat such a culinary chasm. Nor do I rebut his position on the universal local preference for dough burgers by way of asking for his take on the slugs served six blocks away at Nell's. Instead, I hightail it for Weeks Café.

Spend a few days wandering about northeastern Mississippi, eating slug burgers and dough burgers in towns like Corinth and Booneville, Iuka and Baldwyn, not to mention across the Tennessee state line up around Selmer and Savannah, and, soon enough, someone with an appreciation for a good yarn—and a taste for disks of soy meal and ground beef, fried in shallow oil and served between shingles of anemic white bread—will point the way back to Weeks Café, a prefabricated metal building, outfitted with barred windows, and perched on concrete blocks at the edge of a weed-choked hollow.

Willie Weeks is a fifty-something-year-old with a headbanger's mop of gray hair. His face seems to be always creased by a slightly bemused smile, the net effect of which is that he looks to be ever ponderous, even when slicing onions. Along with his wife, Dianne, Willie has dished up burgers here since 1980, when, after a post-college stint in Memphis, he returned to Booneville to take over the family business from his mother, Lois, soon after his father died. "It's kind of like running a beauty salon," he says when asked about daily life behind the grill. "I listen to what people tell me and I do for them what they need."

Willie considers himself to be a student of what he calls old-fashioned hamburgers, a curator of family history who, given half a chance, will reel off the story of his father, Fate, and his four uncles, all of whom operated hamburger stands in or near Corinth. "My daddy was the youngest, the first one to leave Corinth, and the only one to set up shop in Booneville," Willie tells me. "John Weeks was the oldest, the one we believe came home from Chicago sometime around 1919 with a special recipe for hamburgers." Certain versions of the tale pay homage to a German immigrant who gave the family recipe to John. Others incorporate a layover at the St. Louis World's Fair of 1904.

Unlike some local operators, Willie does not serve an all-beef burger. In deference to his forebears, he sticks by his family recipe of beef and soy. As far as he is concerned, *that's* a hamburger. If there's anything aberrant to be pondered, Willie says, it's the now popular use of the term "slug burger" or, more quizzically, the city of Corinth's attempt to leverage the novel appeal of the local delicacy by way of an annual Slug Burger Festival, replete with a sash-swagged Slug Burger Queen and a state fair–style midway chockablock with Tilt-A-Whirls. "Plus, that beef tallow stinks," he says. "It'll clog up your drain and stink up your restaurant."

While Willie slices out blobs of burger mix, cutting them into near perfect rounds with the edge of his spatula, and shoveling them into a shallow pool of oil where they will burble until done, we talk. Along the way, we decide that slug burgers and dough burgers are probably related and that dough burgers are, more than likely, a second generation take on what the Weeks men have been serving all along.

We meander, in a desultory way, toward a shared conclusion that, despite the Weeks family claim to provenance, soy-cut slug burgers and flour-cut dough burgers and, for that matter, meatloaves, are nothing more—and nothing less—than ingenious adaptations by home cooks and grill cooks. Confronted with war or, more recently, poverty, they made do with less meat than they might have liked. "Daddy always chose places where working folks would gather," says Willie, with what might be construed as pride. "He would always set up a burger stand near a courthouse or a cotton gin. He knew how to feed poor people, he knew what they wanted, what they needed."

Careful readers will note that I have not passed judgment on the taste of these burgers. I do not describe the mouth feel of a dough burger or the crunch of a well-fried slug burger. The truth is, after sampling thirteen burgers over three days, I cannot claim to have tasted a single burger that I liked.

But, in the final analysis, who cares what I think; local taste trumps all. In other words, what gives me, a resident of the town that once shunned Box Head's Burgers, the right to pass judgment on local taste? If the good people of Booneville clamor for the slug burgers dished up by Willie Weeks, what right have I to argue otherwise?

Blair's Extend-A-Burgers

While I never warmed to the taste of the slug burgers and dough burgers of northeastern Mississippi, I do recall with fondness the bread-cut burgers served by Fincher's Barbecue of Macon, Georgia. And I've heard positive reports from those patrons of the Snappy Lunch in Mount Airy, North Carolina, who manage to forgo one of their stunningly good slaw-and-chili-swamped pork chop sandwiches in favor of what locals call a breaded hamburger. In other words, the marriage of beef and extender need not be untenable. Some variants on the theme call to mind a meatloaf sandwich. My favorite comes from the keen mind and palate of my wife, Blair. Oatmeal is her secret. And if you still blanch at the thought, you may refer to it as a squashed meatball sandwich.

- 2½ pounds ground chuck
- 1 onion, chopped fine
- 2 garlic cloves, chopped fine
- 2 tablespoons Worcestershire sauce
- 1 teaspoon salt
- 1 tablespoon black pepper
- 1 cup quick-cooking oatmeal
- 2 eggs, beaten

(continued)

- 10 buns
- Mayonnaise
- Lettuce
- Tomato slices
- Pickles

Mix all ingredients together and form into 10 patties. Heat a pan over medium-high heat and cook the burgers for about 3 minutes on each side (for medium-rare). Garnish buns with mayonnaise, lettuce, tomato, and pickles. *Serves 10*

Fairy-Tale Burgers

I n 1899, just as hamburgers were becoming a part of our national diet and our national lexicon, a reporter for the *Daily Herald* of Ohio delineated the compounds—Freezine, Preservatine, Freez-'Em—that unsavory butchers used to extend the shelf life of suspect ground beef. He quoted a leading medical authority of the day who declaimed the chemicals as "disastrous on the tissue of the stomach."

In 1906, Upton Sinclair's muckraking novel *The Jungle* fanned the flames of public distrust with its unflinching depictions of unkempt Chicago packinghouses. One contemporary journalist, clued in to the practice of grinding any and all scraps into ground beef, argued, "the garbage can is where the chopped meat sold by most butchers belongs, as well as a large percentage of all the hamburger that goes into sandwiches."

Billy Ingram and Walt Anderson, founders of the White Castle chain, recognized the problem. Ingram proclaimed that White Castle was different, that the "day of the dirty, greasy hamburger is past . . . for a new system has arisen, the 'White Castle System.'" Ingram and Anderson communicated their message of cleanliness in a number of ways. The name itself broadcast their intent. White signified purity at a time when many stands were dumps. Castle denoted permanence in a day when many stands were fly-by-night affairs.

White Castle also developed a signature architectural style, with crenellated walls and turrets, reminiscent of fairy-tale dreams. They ground the meat and grilled the burgers within sight of their customers. And in a 1930 marketing master-stroke that would prefigure the month-long all-McDonald's diet Morgan Spurlock made infamous in the film *Super Size Me,* White Castle commissioned the physiological chemistry department at the University of Minnesota to determine the nutritional efficacy of an all-burger diet. According to Ingram:

> We arranged for a medical student to live for thirteen weeks on nothing but White Castle hamburgers and water. The student maintained good health throughout the three-month period, and was eating twenty to twenty-four hamburgers a day during the last few weeks.
>
> A food scientist signed a report that a normal, healthy child could eat nothing but our hamburgers and water, and fully develop all its physical and mental faculties if we were to do two things: increase the percentage of calcium in the buns to aid in the development of bone structure, and maintain a specific proportion of bun and patty to provide the correct balance of proteins, carbohydrates, and fats.

Of course, White Castle soon upped the calcium and began trumpeting its burgers as health-giving, even life-affirming. Sales soared. And in White Castle's wake came a flock of imitators, including White Tower, White Palace, White Turret, and White Fortress; White House, White Hut, White Tavern, White Kitchen, and White Wonder; Red Castle, Blue Castle, Silver Castle, and Castle Blanca. Even Stake and Shake, the 1934-vintage midwestern-based chain, was first known as White-house Steak and Shake.

In time, the cumulative effect of good salesmanship and company policy had their desired effects. Burgers—as served by White Castle, or any of the hundreds of other followers of similar creeds—were no longer suspect. They were lunch. Or dinner. And by this point in the story, each component of the iconic burger was in place: patty, bun, mustard, and onions; sometimes ketchup, sometimes pickles. Only the cheese was yet to come.

the
dairy
chronicles

Birth of the Yellowburger

t he origins of the cheeseburger are murky. Lionel Sternberger of the Rite Spot in Pasadena, California, was a
claimant. His advocates peg the date as early as 1924 and as
late as 1926. Perhaps he was a catalyst. By 1928, O'Dell's Fine
Foods of Los Angeles was serving cheeseburgers that, according to a surviving menu, came smothered in chili.

Of course, such evidence trumps previous petitioners to
the grail like Luis Ballast, proprietor of the Humpty Dumpty
Drive-In of Denver, Colorado, who, based upon a 1935 inven-
tion date, petitioned for trademark protection; or Margaret
Kaelin of Louisville, Kentucky, who said she first wed a cheese
sandwich and a hamburger in 1934.

Eventually, some researcher will establish a baseline cheese-burger. One place to start will be with the so-called Memphis Cheeseburger Trial of 1938, during which W. W. Stevens of Dallas sued the Toddle House chain for infringing upon his trademarked cheeseburger. Attorneys for Toddle House coun-tered by showcasing early usage of the term—and of synonyms like yellowburger—to prove that Stevens never was the sole purveyor, let alone the originator. They also described, in mouthwatering detail, how, by 1913, an Illinois restaurant was making cheeseburgers of ground beef and Limburger.

Until then we can take solace in certainties. We seekers of burger lore know, with a reasonable degree of accuracy, that William Taylor, proprietor of Biff's Coffee Shops of California, invented the rye bread–encased patty melt in the late 1940s. More importantly, *I* know that J. C. Reynolds, who operated the Dairy Bar in Columbia, South Carolina, from 1932 to 1984, is the man who popularized the pimento burger.

Proselytizing for
Pimento Burgers

i 'm a proselytizer for pimento burgers. Over the course of
the past few years, I've won many converts. I'm proudest
of my West Coast conquest: Out in San Francisco, Bob Kantor
of Memphis Minnie's bowed to my harangue and began
slathering the good stuff on his burgers.

And he's not the only one. Over in Birmingham, my friends
at Jim 'N Nick's did more than merely acquiesce; they named
a bacon-and-pimento-crowned burger after me. Back home,
Randy Yates of Ajax Diner on the Oxford square no longer
looks askance when I ask him to marry his jalapeño-spiked pimento cheese sandwich and his burger; he just serves it forth.

Yet Columbia, South Carolina, is the true citadel of pimento burgers. In Columbia, pimento burgers are a birthright.
Every third joint serves one; and at least half of them are

good. During my college days, I even considered migrating. Although I claimed otherwise, the true issue was of pimento burger access.

Of late, I've come to believe that it's just as well that I balked. If I lived in close proximity to such a surfeit of goodness, my obsession might dissipate. And that wouldn't do. Soon, I would lose touch with the Columbia titans. I might even quit calling Eddie's on Assembly Street, declaring myself to be a health department inspector and demanding to know what brand of mayonnaise they use.

nd so I remain in Mississippi. The distance suits me: from this remove I can focus. I can track down stories about variants like the psychoburger, an egg-crowned pimento burger once popular with drink-addled University of South Carolina coeds. I can perform experiments, like crowning a filet mignon with pimento cheese as they do at Mr. Friendly's in Columbia's Five Points neighborhood.

I can plot the extents of the phenomenon by way of Curly burgers, long a favorite at the Dairy-O in Orangeburg, South Carolina; Winky Dinky hot dogs from the Penguin in Charlotte, North Carolina, topped with pimento cheese and chili; and, closer to home, the pimento cheese–dressed Palm Beach burgers served at Memphis's Gridiron diners since the days of Elvis.

At home, I lean back in my swivel chair, conjure a pimento burger map, and ruminate on various theories—like the one that a listener to South Carolina historian Walter Edgar's radio show shared with me, the one that is likely to raise the hackles of proud Georgians. He told me that Nancy Simms—current proprietor of the "world's largest drive-in," the Varsity in Atlanta—was not working in a vacuum when she came up with the idea of swabbing burgers with pimento cheese and toasting them in a sandwich press. According to this informant, Simms may have learned the virtues of pimento burgers while a college student in Columbia.

Sequestered in my office, I replay my expeditions to Columbia. My dates with pimento burgers unfold like beloved home movies, jerky and skewed but deeply satisfying: Maurice's Piggy Park. The Salty Nut. Edisto Market. Rockaway's. Palmetto Sandwich Shop. Harper's. The Mousetrap. What A Burger. And, of course, Eddie's, where the picture comes into focus long enough for me to recall the pickle juice that enlivened their pimento cheese. Not a bum pimento burger in the bunch, I tell myself, as the credits roll.

At home in Oxford, I indulge in supporting research, like tracing the origin and diffusion of pimento cheese itself. I track the circa 1910 introduction of canned American pimentos to the Southern market. I plumb old cookbooks for recipes, isolating early renditions like sandwiches of almonds, cheese, and pimentos from *Practical Ideas in Cookery*, published in 1912 by the Presbyterial Institute of Blackshear, Georgia. (And I claim minor victories: With such a cookbook in hand, I can establish that my preferred spelling—pimento, not the more formal pimiento—has long been popular.)

———

W orking the phones, I collect stories from eaters who were lucky enough to know J. C. Reynolds, the original owner of Columbia's Dairy Bar. When talk turns to pimento burgers, his name is always invoked.

Reynolds was a dapper man of slight build, who earned his reputation by churning his own ice cream, and cemented his legacy by dishing up what Edgar and others believe to be the first pimento burger—a thin, diner-style patty, sopped in chili, served on a pimento cheese–daubed bun.

Like thousands of cooks who once toiled at greasy spoons, Reynolds lived in comparative obscurity. Of his mettle I know this: He was a proud member of the working class, a man who earned his keep by the sweat of his brow. If he hadn't been walking the duckboards from 1932 to 1984, he might have been a butcher or a baker, maybe a taxi driver.

Alumni of the University of South Carolina remember Reynolds as a spatula-wielding father figure who dished what the situation required. His food was a balm for the bilious, a benediction for the jilted. Arrive at noon, hungover from a night of debauchery, and he prescribed a pimento burger. Grab a stool at four in the afternoon, tell him your boyfriend just dumped you, and his remedy was the same—a burger adrift in chili and pimento cheese.

Though he looms in many a patron's memory, Reynolds worked the griddle in an age before most journalists deemed his kind to be worthy of copy. Numerous newspaper accounts survive from the 1980s, documenting the fight waged by his successor, Jack Provost, to keep the Dairy Bar open. But there are few public accounts of J. C. Reynolds's life at the grill— nothing but a few yellowed newspaper clippings and a curious bit of videotape. The latter, shot in the late 1980s, was conceived as a marketing vehicle by an entrepreneur intent upon selling the pimento burger to the big guns of the industry.

Whoever made the film scored it with classical music when rockabilly would have been more suitable. And though the narrator speaks, in stentorian tones, of the pimento burger, viewers never actually lay eyes on one. Nor do they get a glimpse of Reynolds at the grill, spatula in hand. Instead they see Reynolds, in a cardigan and tie, posed in front of various Columbia landmarks, like the South Carolina statehouse and Williams-Brice stadium.

Perhaps I shouldn't complain. After all, if the filmmaker had gotten it right, my crusade on behalf of the pimento burger would be needless. As it is, I have much work to do, many converts to win.

PC Burgers

Throughout much of the South, pimento cheese is commonly served one of two ways: stuffed in the hollows of celery stalks and passed as cocktail food, or spread on sliced white bread and eaten as a sandwich. These are simple, almost ascetic; not so this burger. It's a molten stack of meat and goo. It's also delicious. One note: Don't upset the tremulous balance of condiments. Don't ladle on chili like they did at the Dairy Bar. And stay the hand of friends and family who reach for ketchup and mustard. Trust me, you have all you need, smack dab in that pimento cheese.

- 24 ounces extra sharp cheddar, shredded
- 1 (4 oz.) jar diced pimentos, drained
- 1 teaspoon dried, rubbed sage
- 1 tablespoon black pepper
- 2 tablespoons scallions, chopped
- Pinch of sugar (more to taste)
- ⅓ cup mayonnaise

Combine the cheese, drained pimentos, sage, black pepper, scallions, and sugar in a large mixing bowl. Stir in the mayonnaise and work into a chunky paste. Chill the pimento cheese if not using right away. Remove the pimento cheese from the refrigerator before you start cooking the burgers—it needs a few minutes to soften. You will have a lot of pimento cheese left over, which is, after all, the point.

- 4 basic burgers (see recipe on page 174)
- 4 buns

Slather the buns with pimento cheese, add the patties and sheaths of lettuce, maybe slices of tomato. *Serves 4*

Rattling Skeletons and Cheese

i n *The Cheese Handbook,* esteemed British author T. A. Layton offers a recipe that, to most any American, will seem curious:

"Take, per person, two ounces of raw mince meat, one egg yolk, and one segment processed cheese. . . . Bind the meat with the egg, season with salt and pepper, and flatten out to the diameter of a bun. . . . Get a slice of cheese to fit the flattened mince meat and smear with mustard. Put the other bit of mince meat on top. Crimp the edges together and toast under a hot grill. . . ."

Natives of Minneapolis might recognize that Layton, who penned his book in the 1960s, was an advocate of what they know as a Jucy Lucy. Of course, there are some differences. True Jucys aren't slathered with mustard. And the meat in a Jucy is ground finely enough to bind without egg.

But the linkages are there. All that remains to be settled is this: Did Layton fly through Minneapolis on a cheese buyer's junket and return home with a purloined recipe? Or do the folks at Matt's Bar have British skeletons rattling about in their cupboard?

FIVE

Lessons in
Fluid Dynamics

i t's dark in Matt's, a corner bar in the Powderhorn neighborhood of Minneapolis. So dark that I can feel but not see the gold velour wallpaper. After a moment, my eyes adjust and I take a seat. From a barstool perch by the door, I join my friend Dara Moskowitz and gaze upon the objects of our obsession: eight burgers, arranged in two rows.

They pop and hiss, spewing grease onto the grill cook's forearms. He does not flinch. When he flips them, the burger at bottom right begins to wobble, ballooning outward and then quaking like a capsized turtle. Remember *Alien*? It's not unlike that. If you missed Sigourney Weaver's money shot, I'll be more precise: it's as if something is trapped inside that burger; it's as if that something wants out.

Finally a minor geyser erupts, a thin stream of cheese

spouting upward in a textbook exhibition of fluid dynamics. I hear a treble-register swish, an exhalation. And I watch as a blob of cheese exits the side of the burger. What was once a misshapen and lovely thing now resembles nothing so much as a naked Quarter Pounder coming down the chute at McDonald's. I learn, from a woman seated two stools down, that I have witnessed what Jucy Lucy cultists know as a blowout.

a s you have no doubt discerned, a Jucy Lucy is a burger stuffed with cheese. The mechanics, as practiced by the grill cook at Matt's, appear simple: Lay out a shingle of sandwich tissue. Plop a bun-sized patty on top. Drape it with a slice of American cheese. Piggyback with a second patty and a second tissue. Rotate the burger in the palm of your hand, tucking and creasing to seal the seam as you go. Strip the tissues away and toss on a griddle. Cook, and top with grilled onions.

Its shape notwithstanding, a Jucy looks banal, appears humdrum. But believe me, this cheeseburger possesses the ability to astonish. For if you manage to avoid a blowout, you will, upon first bite, taste a cheeseburger that does not follow accepted protocols, but takes its cues from the choicer contents of a Whitman's Sampler box—say, a caramel-gorged fez of dark chocolate.

And if, like me, you notice the bumper stickers that plaster the back bar, the ones that say, "Fear the Cheese," and you figure they have something to do with a football rivalry with Wisconsin, think again. If you bite soon after your Jucy arrives, you will learn—as a sluice of hot cheese product dribbles down your chin—that this burger also possesses the ability to blister.

When my cheeseburger arrives, Dara, known for her discursive restaurant reviews in the local newsweekly, looks toward the grill cook. He appears amused, maybe a bit mischievous. He asks her, "Does he know the rules?"

By this point, the onion-scented cloud, which followed my Jucy from the griddle to the counter, has begun to dissipate. I check the surface for breaks, determine that I have not received a blowout, and hoist my Jucy aloft. But Dara stays my hand. "Give it a while," she says, pointing toward the bumper stickers. I frown and order another beer.

It's not as if I'm hungry. I've spent the better part of the past two days traversing Wisconsin and Minnesota, eating and deconstructing cheeseburgers in an attempt to establish a read on this corner of the Midwest.

I began on the north side of Milwaukee, in the neighborhood of Glendale. At Solly's Grille, set in a faux Victorian home within sight of the interstate, I met Glenn Fieber, stepson of Solly, keeper of the butter burger flame. I put to rest any doubts that eats hereabouts might be no different from, say, Corinth, Mississippi, when I lifted the top bun from my burger with cheese and found not one pat of butter—not even two— but a creamy hummock of the stuff. When I asked Fieber why, he said, absent a trace of irony, "That's how we do it."

Though he may be the most extravagant practitioner of the art, Fieber is no renegade butter pimp. All across Wisconsin, I encountered his ilk. At Mazo's Fine Foods in Milwaukee proper. At the ninety-odd locations of the Culver's chain, scattered across the state. At Kroll's West, across the street from Lambeau Field in Green Bay. Indeed, the butter burger phenomenon has spread so far and wide that Bert Vaux, a professor of linguistics at the University of Wisconsin—Milwaukee, has begun a dialect survey to determine extents and influence.

Just across the state line in Miesville, Minnesota (pop. 135), I discovered an aberration worthy of a footnote in Vaux's study. At King's Place, a clapboard roadhouse across the street from St. Joseph's Catholic Church, I ate a hand-patted burger layered with Swiss, cheddar, and pepper jack cheeses that, thanks to a slather of sour cream—and my own predisposition toward seeing good in most every embellishment—I found to be almost wholesome, in the manner of a baked potato. It helped when I learned that the sour cream was not a fit of excess, but the ovum-intolerant owner's substitute for mayonnaise.

By the time I arrived at Vincent, an au courant Minneapolis restaurant operated by a Frenchman who earned his stripes at New York's four-star Le Bernardin, I was already pining for a Jucy Lucy. But research called. And Dara had said good things about their interpretation of Daniel Boulud's now iconic braised short rib and foie gras–stuffed burger. I should not have fretted. For in what I've come to consider a shotgun marriage of Daniel and Lucy, the chef at Vincent had, from the get-go, used not foie gras but cheese. Smoked Gouda, to be exact.

i am telling Dara about my lunch at Vincent's, when she gives the all-clear on my Jucy Lucy. I'm unsure whether she has grown weary of my cheeseburger tales or whether the danger has truly passed, but I don't seek clarification; I just bite. Turns out, Dara gauged the wait about right. The cheese is hot but not scalding, fluid but no longer propulsive. I take another bite and fall quiet.

To tell the truth, my burger is far less complex than I imagined. I don't mean to discount the skill of the grill man. Or the architectural ingenuity of the cook who first calculated the proper ratio of beef to cheese. But I had anticipated a taste that would upend my cheeseburger paradigm. It does not.

In 1954, when local legend holds that the first Jucy Lucy came off a griddle at Matt's, the notion of crimping a slice of cheese inside two patties was novel. But five decades hence, a Jucy seems merely quirky. Only the texture of the cheese confounds.

Nowadays, Connecticut barrooms peddle Brie-girded burgers. And Phoenix mini-marts vend feta burgers on wheated pita for the low carb–inclined. And New Orleans taverns serve deep-fried burgers, which, when cut across the bias, reveal the constituent ingredients in a club sandwich.

In other words, the burger is no longer merely provincial. Or parochial. Or any of those other p-words. It's liberated. And in the wake of such liberation, we Americans have a habit of returning to the old verities. Fifty years out, the Jucy Lucy can be appreciated as quirky and local. And by dint of this alone, the Jucy is worthy of celebration.

Maybe, just maybe, the real pleasure of eating such a burger in the year 2004 is in taking a seat at a dim bar of storied provenance and listening to someone tell you about how their hometown favorite was born. In the case of the Jucy, this is what Cheryl Bristol, daughter of founder Matt Bristol, told Dara:

"There was a bachelor customer who used to come in every day and order a burger. One day . . . he told the cook to seal up some cheese in the middle. So the cook did, and when he bit into it, the hot cheese spurted out, and he wiped his mouth and said, 'Oooh, that's one juicy Lucy!'" When Dara asked the significance of the name, probing for a link to a salty barmaid or a kindly grandmother, Cheryl just told her, "They used to talk goofy like that back then."

As for why the "i" in juicy was subsequently dropped, that's a mystery for the ages. One thing, however, is for sure: the dropped vowel has become a differentiating factor. I went to four other barrooms that served cheese-stuffed burgers. Whether in recognition of Matt's status as originator or in remembrance of a particularly stern grade-school spelling teacher, all included the "i."

I Love Jucy Lucy

Don't reach for a hunk of your best cheddar. Don't even reach for real cheese. A slice of processed American cheese, specifically the kind packaged in those plastic sleeves, is the preferred stuffing for this burger. Only those orange squares of vaguely plastic texture will achieve the proper fluidity. Now that I've liberated you from the constraints of so-called good taste, allow me to caution you: Cheez Whiz is, at least as far as this recipe goes, beyond the bounds of propriety.

- 1½ pounds ground chuck
- 1 tablespoon Worcestershire sauce
- ¾ teaspoon garlic salt
- 1 teaspoon black pepper
- 4 slices American cheese

- 4 buns
- Condiments and garnishes of your choice

Combine the beef with Worcestershire sauce, salt, and pepper, and mix well. Divide into 8 portions. Make thin round patties, broader than the cheese slices. Place a

(continued)

a cheese slice onto 4 of the patties. Top each piece of cheese with a remaining patty. Press the edges together very well to seal. Prepare a medium-hot charcoal fire and cook for 3–4 minutes per side for a medium burger. Place on buns and dress with your favorite garnishes and condiments. *Serves 4*

Keep Your Hat On

While in Minneapolis, I not only get a taste of a propulsive Jucy Lucy, I get a gleaning of the way cheeseburgers must have tasted sixty or seventy years ago. At the circa 1939 Band Box, the surviving location in a local chain, I take a seat at grill level and eat one of those thin pucks that owes its evanescence not to the quality of the cheese or the skill of the cook, but to the heady porosity of a grill in service since the Roosevelt administration.

The real payoff comes in conversation with a man who might be the owner. He tells me that the name refers to a thin wood box in which hatbands or detachable collars would have been kept. In common usage of the time, however, the term came to mean "exquisitely neat, clean or ordered."

It's likely that the folks who started the Band Box were inspired by the success of other chains, like White Castle and its ken, which, in the days when burger houses were considered eateries of ill repute, sought to evoke the sanitary gleam of a well-scrubbed and wholesome kitchen.

A less disingenuous path to respectability might have been to address the nimbus of grease that oftentimes floated above the grill. Come to think of it, if the Band Box folks had adopted the steamed cheeseburger chests of Connecticut as their own, they might have lived up to the conceit.

Mapping a Microclimate

When French oenologists talk of wine, they often speak of microclimates, of faraway places where soil and sun and a host of other environmental variables conspire in such a way that cabernet franc vines thrive or botrytis fungi find their noble prey. And when they talk, we educated eaters and drinkers know of what they speak.

Closer to home, we recognize similar variables and equally sublime possibilities in corners of America where, come spring, ramps shoot through the humus of an Appalachian vale, or, come fall, coral-hued chicken of the woods mushrooms blanket the Cascade foothills. But we have heretofore overlooked cheeseburger microclimates.

Consider for a moment the peculiar triangle of south-central Connecticut, bound roughly on the west by Meriden, on the east by Middletown, and on the south by Wallingford. Here and only here is the fabled steamed cheeseburger, or, more colloquially, the steamer, found in abundance.

You can't discern the steamer microclimate by analyzing the forage that local cattle graze. The few cows found hereabouts provide neither meat nor cheese for steamers. No, the secret is a stainless steel box of the type marketed as the Burg'r Tend'r or the New England Cheeseburger Chest by Daleco, a Wallingford company doing business in Bob Gattilia's basement. Within such a box, within the stainless steel confines of that squat chest, a Connecticut cheeseburger microclimate blossoms.

i saw my first cheeseburger chest a couple years back at Ted's, a four-stool joint in Meriden. It was the color of a dull nickel, and it rested on a burner at the bottom right corner of the stove. A squall of steam encircled the box. It reminded me of a personal sauna, the kind in which, if my memory of Movietone Newsreels serves, flapper-era Hollywood moguls stewed and smoked cigars.

Before I ordered my first steamer, I sat, transfixed, for a good ten minutes. I was enthralled by the box, but I also enjoyed watching the kid behind the counter. He worked quickly, with his head down, his elbows pulled in tight. For each steamer ordered he flicked the box open with his spatula. After a feint to avoid the steam corona that curled his way, he shuffled the trays, working to select ground beef mounds of an optimum firmness and puddles of white cheddar that were sufficiently tremulous. By the time he slapped the contents of

two trays on a Kaiser roll and slid a steamer down the counter
to a waiting customer, it was time to begin again.

I gave him the high sign. Less than a minute passed before
a cheeseburger came skidding my way. The poppy seed roll
was nothing special. But the contents were, in the truest sense
of the word, extraordinary. The burger looked like a slab of
meatloaf, rectangular in shape, loose in consistency, with a
convex crown. And the cheese resembled nothing so much as
fondue. In yellow rivulets, it cascaded down the face of the
burger, splotching my paper plate with pools of butterfat.

b ob Gattilia has heard this all before. A silver-haired retired banker, he is accustomed to picking up the phone
and talking a new convert through the stations of the cross.
But I haven't rung him up. I've knocked at his door. And now,
because he's a gracious man, I'm camped out on his couch,
babbling on about microclimates and butterfat.

If I were he, I would have shown me the door. But the
seventy-something-year-old has an outsized sense of responsibility, typical, in my experience, of Rotary Club members or
Moose Lodge brothers. And as the sole commercial manufacturer of cheeseburger chests, he feels duty-bound to spread
the good word.

We descend the stairs to a carpeted basement. There's a
bar and two stools against the back wall. Shelves stacked with
toy stagecoaches flank the bar; above hangs a stained glass
lamp. Scattered about are beer steins and cheeseburger chest
prototypes and framed testimonials to the virtues of steamed

meat and cheese. Among the testimonials is a poem, "The Magical Box." One of the couplets goes something like this: "This magical box can produce burgers galore/ Delicious burgers that you will adore." (I check the authorship and am relieved to see that Bob didn't write it.)

Bob steers me around the corner, past the washer and dryer, to a stoop-ceilinged workroom where, using a cast-off dining room table as a workbench, he spot-welds his products from die-cut sheets of steel. As he shows me various models— the four-rack twenty-four slotter favored by local diners, the ten-slotter popular with home cooks—we discuss the genesis and evolution of the steamer.

Like most who have given some thought to local fare, Bob talks of the days when lunch wagons were the preferred canteens of factory workers. (This was back in the teens and twenties, when Connecticut was the manufacturing center for cutlery, and Meriden Britannia—not to mention a half dozen other silver plate companies—were running two-shift operations.) In the beginning, vendors cooked burgers at home and stashed them in steam cabinets for the factory trip. Before long, entrepreneurs realized that they didn't need to pre-cook their burgers; they could prepare them on-site.

"This was the ideal place to get something like this going," Bob tells me. "They might have started out cooking their burgers on Dutch ovens fit with a Frisbee pie plate. All they had to do was knock holes in the plate and put a lid top on, and they had a steamer. But since there were so many old tin-knockers around who knew how to work with metal, pretty soon a lot of people were custom-making these boxes."

———

a s we ascend the stairs in search of lunch, I tell Bob about my first trip to Ted's, about my first steamer. Bob looks down at the floor and tells me that he'd rather not go to Ted's. "I think Paul, the owner, is mad at me," says Bob. "I've heard that when people ask him about my chests, he tells them I'm out of business. He thinks I'm some kind of threat."

I feel for Bob; he's hardly primed to put Ted's out of business. In a good year, he might sell two hundred boxes. A few of those two hundred go to Connecticut expatriates, marooned in some godforsaken place like Arizona or Oregon where burgers are fried or broiled or grilled. Sure, there have been brushes with the big time. A few years back, the Subway chain tested a few boxes in their stores. And, yes, there is the occasional query from a fast-talker who claims a fat bankroll and has plans for a fleet of wheeled cheeseburger chests. (Truth be told, the turf war calls to mind the instinct Henry Kissinger explored when, in a discussion of academic politics, he told an audience of educators, "In any dispute, the intensity of feeling is inversely proportional to the value of the stakes at issue.")

For the most part, Bob sells his boxes to the hash houses and drive-ins of the triangle. As a rule, these are not fine dining establishments. "Some of these places," Bob says, cutting his eyes my way, "are real buckets of blood."

When I tell him that I'd rather not come to a complete understanding of what that means, he turns his Buick into the gravel lot of Sara J's, a weather-beaten diner of another sort in

Wallingford. The box that sits on her stove is not a Daleco original. The squat shape is similar, maybe a little taller. The capacity looks about the same, but the exterior is not flat nickel; it's incised with a chevron pattern. Bob steps to the counter and nods toward the box. Karen, the owner, takes him for a restaurant inspector. (I think: Could this be the origin of his supposed ostracism?) But Karen calms when she realizes that all he wants to do is talk steamed cheeseburgers.

Karen and Bob fall into a conversation that I'm pretty sure you won't hear anywhere else: for a good ten minutes they talk of nothing but cheeseburger chests. Bob tells her that some of the early ones were made of cast iron and copper. Karen tells him that her boyfriend, a truck mechanic, had originally planned to cut up a beer keg and use it for the chassis. Bob tells her that, should she ever need them, he sells replacement trays that will likely fit her box.

By the time talk turns to the piano hinges that are the industry standard for chest doors, my burger arrives. At Karen's suggestion, mine is on toast. With extra cheese. And it's as unnervingly good and sloppy and, yes, foreign to my sensibilities as that first steamer at Ted's. The cheese, however, is different. It still has that plasticine texture, that Play-Doh-warmed-in-the-microwave mouth feel. But it tastes sharper than I recall, almost tannic, nearly citric.

After a couple more stops for steamers, Bob and I make our way back to his house. While standing on his stoop, in the process of taking my leave, I bring up the subject of sharpness. Obviously different burger joints are likely to use different cheddars, and all tastes are relative: one man's sharp is another man's extra sharp. But that cheddar at Sarah J's nearly took my head off.

Another steamer cook, whom I met earlier in the day, told me that chests function like "time machines." According to this guy, ten minutes in the chest "speed ages" a cheese. So I ask Bob whether the size of a chest could have an effect on the sharpness of the cheese that emerges. Could it be that as the microclimate in the box varies, so does the sharpness of the steamed cheese?

And I ask him whether, when he uses a Burg'r Tend'r at home, he prefers a ten-slot or a twenty-four-slot model. That's when Bob steps to the side and points his way back into the kitchen. "My wife and I cook our burgers on that," he says gesturing toward a George Foreman Lean Mean Grilling Machine. "And they always come out real nice."

Mug-Steamed Cheese

In his book Serious Pig, *John Thorne offers a breakfast savor that comes close to the texture of Connecticut steamed cheese. For those intent upon replicating the taste of Connecticut at home, this recipe will have to suffice because I've tried—and failed—to steam meat at home. I usually end up with a lump that resembles a crumpled sweat sock. However, when I followed Thorne's recipe for the cheese, it emerged from its steam bath luxuriant and was soon pooling in eddies on top of my burger. If you pine for a fully steamed experience, you might want to ring Bob Gattilia at (203) 269-7333. For a couple hundred dollars, he'll ship you a ten-slot home unit.*

- 16 ounces cheddar cheese, shredded coarsely

- 4 basic burgers (see recipe on page 174)
- 4 sets of buns
- Salt to taste
- Pepper to taste
- Condiments and garnishes of your choice

Fill a coffee mug with half the cheese until it is three-fourths full. Pour boiling water to the rim of the cup and cover with a saucer. Repeat with a second mug, cheese, and water. Stand in a warm place for 10 minutes. Pour off the water and pour the cheese, which will be the consistency of thick cream, on a burger. Sprinkle with salt and pepper and serve with your favorite condiments and garnishes. *Enough for 2 burgers*

Warholian Dreams

S ome burgers serve as vehicles for the conveyance of cal-ories; others serve as vehicles for people. I came to know as much during a conversation with Hamburger Harry, who motors about his adopted hometown of Daytona Beach, Florida, on a three-wheeled burger-shaped motor-trike.

His original prototype featured a bun-shaped chassis stippled with sesame seeds. The effect was pleasing to the eye, said Hamburger Harry Sperl, a German émigré who commissioned the fiberglass burger-shaped bike with ketchup bottle front struts, red onion rounds for rear hubcaps, a dill pickle throttle, a chrome tachometer shaped like a milkshake drum, and a sound system that broadcasts the spatter and hiss of burgers on a flattop.

But there was a problem. When Sperl clambered onto his three-wheeler and leaned forward to grasp the chopper bars, his elbows scraped against the seeds. And he feared that when he cut the wheel while motoring down the beach, the kernels of sesame might chafe him to a pulp. So he removed the seeds from the bun and plastered some on a beige helmet.

Sperl was not happy with the compromise. But he took solace in the vérité of the ground beef patty beneath his seat, in the emerald whorls of fiberglass lettuce and the true-to-form ketchup dollops and the luminous triangles of American cheese peeking from beneath the naked bun. And he knew that, should his denuded Hamburger Harley lose its appeal, he could lay hands on his collection of hamburger-shaped pencil erasers and yo-yos; or fix upon his burger candles and cookie jars; or listen to his ceramic burger-shaped music box. (If I remember correctly, it plays a song that sounds something like "Greensleeves.")

"I was born in the wrong country," he tells me. "I'm an American at heart; my first American car was a 1950 Dodge Stepside. I've always seen myself as American. I love Betty Boop, Mickey Mouse. My collecting could have gone that way, too, could have gone any way American.

"I started out collecting American things like car hop trays," he says as I scan his living room in an effort to mentally catalogue his curiosities. "Back in the late 1980s, when I needed a plastic burger to display on a tray, I bought a squeaky toy at the pet store, one of those burgers that puppies gnaw on. But it wasn't good enough. And neither was the next fake burger I bought. That's what drew me into 3-D collecting; I was looking for the good ones."

Sperl has found his quarry. Sunglasses with burger lenses; burger-shaped phones, radios, and compact disc players. Cookie jars, lamps, and mobiles, arranged on row after regimental row of shelves; wristwatches, key chains, bracelets, and earrings, stocked in backlit jewelry cases: all in the shape of burgers. He's even got a burger waterbed.

Running my hands across burger pillows, hoisting a burger

candle from the shelf, I come to appreciate the burger anew. Sperl helps me see the burger as an artifact, a perfect encapsulation of the American appetite. In the manner of Warhol and his soup cans, I come to see Sperl's burger-shaped squeaky toys as something both mundane and profound.

When I finally do work up the courage to ask Sperl for permission to climb on his burger and ride, he tells me that, at least for the time being, it's no longer a functional sculpture. Until the Harley gets the tune-up it so desperately needs, Sperl says his burger is just art.

local
fare

SEVEN

Fritos, Shypokes,
and Chihuahuas

f resh and seasonal are the catchwords in modern culinary circles, but not all great food requires supplication at the altar of the greenmarket. Sometimes local food is defined in a way that riles gourmet fetishists and goads farm-to-table idealists.

The bean burgers of San Antonio, Texas, are local. Indeed, they are singular. Call for a bean burger elsewhere and you're likely to get a pressed disk of soybeans that tastes like a compound of thatch and tabby. Truth be told, I don't consider veggie burgers worthy of their suffix.

In San Antonio, a bean burger is something else entirely. Popular since at least the 1950s, it's a beef patty embellished with two mass-produced pantry staples held dear by natives of

San Antonio: cans of refried beans and bags of corn chips. Cheez Whiz, the bastard child of skim milk, plays a supporting role. Sure, the beans may have been grown in California. And the corn was likely harvested in Iowa. But those canned and bagged commodities bespeak San Antonio.

m y first taste comes at Good Time Charlie's, a late-night haunt, all smudged windows and sticky tabletops and smoldering ashtrays. When I ask the waitress for a medium-rare burger, she tells me, "We cook 'em all well-done, on account of that Mad Elizabeth Taylor Disease." When I ask her to explain the Irish fries, she says, "Hell if I know, maybe they put kidney pie on top."

I order a bean burger, cooked to whatever temperature she likes. When it arrives, I learn that a talent for sass extends to the kitchen, for, after slathering the heel of my bun with re-fried beans and embedding it with chips, someone saw fit to slip a fried onion ring beneath the patty. I start to call my waitress over and object to this bastardization of the bean and chips norm, but a woman two tables over senses my distress and leans my way. "It's OK, honey," she says, "some people call that a ring burger. Even Sill's would do it that way."

t hat was not the last time I would hear the Sill's name in-voked. Not by a long stretch. Among bean burger lovers, a Sill's Snack Shop citation trumps all. The late and much lamented grill in Alamo Heights is the acknowledged origin

point, the very spot where, in the early 1950s, man first plastered refried beans on a beef patty, crushed a handful of
Fritos into the goo, and cemented the top bun with a smear
of Cheez Whiz. Sill himself, on the other hand, is less likely
to claim authorship; he would tell you that he picked up
the idea from a serviceman stationed at nearby Fort Sam
Houston, but that he improved upon the fellow's recipe—
jettisoning American cheese for Cheez Whiz, the newfangled
sensation of 1953.

Fifty years later, his embellishments can be said to define
the burger as Texan while paying homage to the Mexican roots
of the state's people. Of course, I could be overanalyzing this.
But I'm convinced that his bean burger evokes as strong
a sense of place as cedar-planked salmon from Washington
State's Sammamish Watershed, or Basque barbecue lamb from
Boise, Idaho.

O ver the course of a three-day ramble, I taste many a
bean burger. Good Time Charlie's does not prove to
be a standard-bearer of the tradition. But there are a wealth
of worthy contenders, including Casbeer's, an old beer hall
ringed in Christmas lights. And variations on the theme
abound. Although most cooks use refried pintos, black beans
are gaining at places like EZ's Brick Oven and Grill. Sadly,
some cooks now ignore the unwritten but widely embraced
San Antonio dictate that bean burgers should be unsullied
by a shred of green, and add lettuce. Others are gentle. At
Cappy's, a Chamber of Commerce clubhouse serving wines by

the glass at ten dollars a pop, they navigate such treachery by swabbing the bun with guacamole.

Tostada burgers are everywhere, including at the much venerated Chris Madrid's, a warehouse joint that always seems to clock a best burger rating in the local press. At first blush, Madrid's burger appears to be nothing more—and nothing less—than a bean burger by another name. Refried pintos are de rigueur. Cheese serves as glue. Ketchup is frowned upon.

But the substitution of tortilla chips for Fritos rankles. And so does the name. Tostada burger is too literal, too accurate. Bean burger has the ring of pleasant anachronism, of coinage in the 1950s when Hindus were the folks who swore off beef.

Localized fanaticism is predicated upon peculiar local knowledge. And the term "bean burger" is cryptic enough to inspire a tight fraternity of devotees. Call it a tostada burger and everyone is in on the joke. Ditch the Fritos and, before you know it, the Taco Bell menu developers are on the phone.

for a full day, I stray from my appointed rounds, in a futile search for Little Hipp's, a joint locally famous for its shy-poke eggs—a tortilla dish that, by strategic placement of yellow cheese and white cheese and sliced jalapeños, could, in just the right light, with just the right amount of beer coursing through your veins, resemble fried eggs served sunnyside up.

Instead, I end up hanging with Scudder Miller, proprietor of Billy T's Burger Shoppe. Turns out that he knows shypoke, but he does not brook or cook such folderol. What he does serve is a cheese-draped hot dog, tucked in a tortilla blanket and deep fried—a dish that he calls a red dog and that is known in some San Antonio quarters as a Chihuahua.

Miller is a onetime rock-and-roll drummer who flips patties in a squat wooden building, perched hard by the Austin Highway. The interior of Billy T's is decorated with vintage Jethro Tull and Jefferson Airplane posters. He looks to be in his late forties, and he has the slightly haggard look of a man who was serious about his former profession. Miller plays the stereo loud, even when the Bay City Rollers are in heavy rotation.

His bean burger is a calamity on a plate, sluiced with refried beans, pocked with Fritos. As he serves, he talks theory, and I soon learn that he's the self-anointed inheritor of the Sill's Snack Shop legacy. Of course, we're in agreement about Cheez Whiz. And the Fritos are there, dripping from the back end of my burger, for anyone to see. But Miller does deviate from the accepted dictates laid down back in the fifties. "Frank Sill always used Rosarita brand refried beans," he tells me. "I make my own."

to the people of San Antonio, the bean burger is an artifact, a unique constituency of ingredients. Refried beans are integral—as spackle to bind a tumult of ingredients, as a creamy counterpoint to the greasy blast of the beef patty. And if you forgo mustard and ketchup as old man Sill would have had it, Cheez Whiz serves as an ideal lubricant for the assemblage. But as my time in San Antonio passes—and as I eat more bean burgers— I begin to believe that the true secret may be the Fritos. I'm serious.

The deal is sealed when I learn that, although Fritos have long been distributed nationwide, the brand we know was born in San Antonio, when, in 1932, Elmer Doolin convinced his mother to hock her wedding ring and front him the money to buy a small corn chip maker's route. In other words, piling a mess of Fritos atop the beans can be interpreted as an exercise in regional fealty.

Along the same lines, you're more likely to see a native of Atlanta, Georgia, downing a Coke for breakfast. Or a native of Austin, Minnesota, eating a lunch of fried Spam on toast. Say what you want about fresh, but tastes such as these sure are local.

San Antonio Special

As is the case with the fritas of Miami, my devotion to San Antonio bean burgers is a textural fixation. Yeasty, soft bun, silky refried beans, pooled atop a coin of ground beef. Crisp Fritos. Cheez Whiz in all its Day-Glo glory. Each is integral to the whole, so don't make substitutions, especially in the cheese department. Cheez Whiz may look like plastic, but it fixes Fritos to the bun better than epoxy and tastes a far sight better.

- 1 pound ground chuck
- 1 (8-oz.) can refried beans
- Salt and pepper to taste

- 4 buns
- 1 small (15 oz.) jar Cheez Whiz
- ¼ onion, chopped fine
- Medium-sized bag of Fritos corn chips

Divide the meat into 4 even portions and shape into loose rounds. Place a heavy skillet over medium-high heat for 5 minutes. Dump the contents of the bean can into a saucepan and heat, over medium-high, until burbling. Meanwhile cook the burgers for 3 minutes per side, salting and peppering both sides to taste.

Toast the buns and smear Cheez Whiz on each half. Sprinkle a handful of onions over the heel bun and place the patty on top. Spread the patty with beans, toss a handful or 2 of Fritos on, and clamp the crown bun down.

Viva La Difference *Serves 4*

In Praise of Heterogeneity

"The Golden Arches are now more widely recognized than the Christian cross," wrote Eric Schlosser in *Fast Food Nation.* "The basic thinking behind fast food has become the operational system of today's retail economy, wiping out small businesses, obliterating regional differences, and spreading identical stores throughout the country like a self-replicating code."

If you go by the numbers, Schlosser is spot-on. But I discovered during a year on the road in search of America between the buns that, despite Schlosser's empirical accuracy, his theory is—how should I say this?—anecdotally flawed.

By this I mean that, in this age, McDonald's may be best understood as something other than a restaurant chain. Call it a vendor of commodities, of calorie delivery vehicles. In the real world, in the shadows of those arches, regional differences still thrive. I mean that breadth of the American palate is still evident in the enduring traditions that distinguish our 100-plus-year love affair with sandwiches of ground beef.

Hamburger America, a quiet film released in the summer of 2004 by George Motz, argues the same point. Motz profiles the people behind America's distinctive burgers, functioning as a kind of cinematic palliative to Schlosser's jeremiad. He turns his camera on some of the same places I visited, including Ted's, the steamed cheeseburger king of Connecticut; Solly's Grille, home of the Wisconsin butter burger; and Bobcat Bite, purveyor of green-chile cheeseburgers, pride of Santa Fe, New Mexico.

EIGHT

Copping a Chile Buzz

ockroaches avoid cupboards where chiles are stored. Rats don't chew electrical cables coated in habanero pulp. Roadrunners don't peck at fenceposts impregnated with pulverized piquins. And human beings spend tens of millions of dollars annually on chile peppers and chile pepper derivatives, fiery products with inviting names like Crying Tongue, Colon Cleanser, and Kiss Your Ass Goodbye.

Until fairly recently, I was suspicious. Sure, I knew that chiles are chock-full of capsaicin, a chemical compound that, when ingested, kindles a fireball. And I knew that many people savor such an experience because, soon after the fireball ignites, our immune systems counter with a charge of endorphins, those pleasure-giving, balm-inducing, natural opiates.

I understood the chemistry, but I didn't understand the

cult. Observed from a distance, these chile heads were not a pretty lot. Thumbing through copies of *Chile Pepper* magazine, I marveled at barrel-gutted women in jalapeño-print bathing suits, wearing armadillo tiaras. And I watched television coverage of a chile pepper convention, showcasing a new brand of salsa that was said to register in the upper reaches of the Scoville scale. It worked like this: Each taster signed a waiver, holding the manufacturer harmless for damages. Then he—it was almost always a he—scooped a dainty portion of salsa on a chip and bit. After swallowing, the man recoiled in horror and went windmilling through the building, yelping and screeching like a Pentecostal preacher consumed in a fit of glossolalia.

I was not impressed. That's not to say I'm fire averse. I like Tabasco on my scrambled eggs. I'm a fool for Szechuan-style shrimp. And I'm an Ethiopian wat-sopper from way back. But if I'm looking to get happy, I'll mix a drink. What's wrong with bourbon when it's cold, gin when it's hot?

in Santa Fe, New Mexico, a high plains citadel of brown adobe, I discover that chiles are more than mere components in a tongue- and mind-numbing sauce. They are totems. Come winter, ristras of sun-dried peppers hang from Christmas trees like garland. Come summer, teenagers buckboard through arroyos on ATVs, trailing ristras from their handlebars.

And, yes, here chiles are commerce. All year long, tourists throng the shops on the plaza, buying chile-decked coffee mugs, oven mitts, and aprons; chile-shaped champagne flutes, martini glasses, and vases; chile-spiked pancake mix, peanut brittle, and pretzels.

But chiles figure largest in everyday life. They matter most when applied to everyday food. Breakfast burritos burst with magmas of crumbled bacon and green chiles; bowls of posole swirl with angry eddies of red chiles; and, of course, burgers arrive at table awash in green chiles.

I eat flattop-fried cheeseburgers at a humble adobe joint called Dave's Not Here and relish the hippie-appeasing whole wheat bun and the hot ramekin of green chiles served alongside. I order a burger *divorciado* at Horseman's Haven, a onetime gas station dependency, and learn that such a preparation—one side chili, one side salsa—is better saved for eggs. And I make a long detour to the Owl Bar in San Antonio, New Mexico, where I scarf a green chile cheeseburger while listening to locals tell stories of the first atomic bomb test in 1945, when the coyotes turned white with shock and the sky turned blood red.

In other words, I'm no greenhorn when I take a seat at Tomasita's, a Greek-owned fount of New Mexican–style cookery, long popular in Santa Fe. Although I am tempted, I pass on the beef-stuffed sopaipillas and the egg-crowned cheese enchiladas (each available with red chile, green chile, or Christmas chile—which means a little of each) and I beeline for the burger. Iggy Patsalis, the proprietor, bills it as a Super Tortilla Burger, which translates onto the plate as a puck of beef, tucked in a flour tortilla, smothered with refried beans, melted cheese, and—of course—chiles.

It's delicious, a paragon of the form. After I polish mine off, I wipe a thin bead of sweat from my brow, and track Iggy down in the kitchen. Ten minutes of banter follow, during which I alternately praise his burger and ask whether he has ever had an occasion to travel to San Antonio, Texas, land of the bean burger. In the end we agree that his chile cheeseburger is sui generis; and, as a consolation prize, Iggy hands me a box of baklava for the road.

I'm in the car, rifling through my notes, trying to get a handle on my day, when a mild buzz sneaks up on me. Drink two beers in quick succession and you'll have an inkling of how I feel. To be fair, I've noticed this sensation a couple times over the course of the past few days, but there were always extenuating circumstances. If I felt a buzz in the morning, while eating my green chile enchiladas, I chalked it up to coffee. And if I got a little light-headed in the afternoon while downing my green chile cheeseburger, I blamed it on the beer.

But this is different. I am under the influence of neither stimulant nor depressant. And come to think of it, those peppers were pretty hot. (Not as hot as the ones at Horsemen's Haven, but fiery nonetheless.) Could this dreamy gauze that clouds my eyes be chile-induced? Could it be that I am under the influence of endorphins?

I fight off the whelming urge to nap and pilot the car south out of town, toward the Bobcat Bite, famous since 1953 for two-fister chile cheeseburgers. If this were a normal day, I would be anxious, drumming my fingers on the dashboard, fiddling with the radio, running through facts about the next destination in my head, but the chile balm is with me. So I sing along to bad songs on the radio until I coast into the washboard parking lot.

Once inside the plank-shod building, I peruse a shelf loaded down with Snickers bars and hypnotherapy brochures and bird watching manuals before taking a seat at the counter in front of a massive plateglass window. The Overlook Mountain Range towers in the near distance. Ten feet beyond the window, two birds twitter amongst the branches of a piñon.

In due course, my burger comes, a ten-ouncer, extra green chile on the side. I take a bite, and then another. It's as great as everyone told me it would be, charred on the outside, a rosy medium-rare within. About then, a third bird arcs into the piñon, and I reach for *Birds of the Southwest, Volume One.* And as I nibble at my side order of chiles, I focus every bit of mental energy I can muster on deciding whether those flapping wings belong to titmice or Oregon juncos.

The next morning, on my way to the airport, I pull into a McDonald's for a cup of coffee. The chiles have worn off and I'm back to my usual jitters. A special value meal catches my eye. There it is, number 11 on the drive-through menu, a green chile double cheeseburger with fries and a Coke. I shove five bucks toward the order window and rev the engine on my four-banger rental.

I find the green chiles nestled among the pickle chips.

They lack real heat, endorphin-inducing heat, but they pack resonance.

I want to believe that this riff is the work of a renegade McDonald's franchisee. But I know it's actually part of a calculated strategy. Like the Catholic Church, McDonald's does not denounce the religions it displaces; it deifies their saints. I've seen it all across the country. In south Alabama where barbecue is the thing, McDonald's trots out the McRib. In south Florida, they dish McCubanos. Up next, in Berkeley, California, the heirloom tomato–topped McAliceWaters.

Chile Buzzburger

I had one problem with the burger at Tomasita's: it was impossible to pick up and eat out of hand. In my book, burgers are meant to be handled. But the lava that Iggy ladles on forced me to do battle with knife and fork. After I returned home, I made a few adjustments. A trip to the Mexican bodega up the street inspired the substitution of queso blanco (Mexican melting cheese) for standard-issue American. And since I wasn't going to blanket my burger in beans, I added a bit of salsa verde for moisture. I'm hoping Iggy won't be mad.

- ⅛ head iceberg lettuce, chopped
- 1 tomato, chopped
- 1 large onion, chopped fine
- Salsa verde to taste
- 4 ounces green chiles, diced (Try to get your hands on fresh or frozen ones from Hatch, New Mexico. Failing that, substitute canned green chiles.)
- 1 pound ground chuck
- 1 teaspoon salt
- 1 teaspoon pepper
- 4 ounces queso blanco cheese, sliced
- 4 large tortillas

In a bowl, mix lettuce, tomato, and half the onion with salsa verde. Combine as you would a salad and set aside. In another bowl, toss half the chiles and the other half of the onions with the meat. Add salt and pepper. Form the mixture into 4 patties and set aside. Over a medium-high charcoal fire, cook the burgers for 2 or 3 minutes per side, adding cheese after you flip. Remove burgers from heat. Add the rest of the chiles, and press until they adhere to the cheese. Set aside.

Working over the charcoal, toast tortillas on each side until they begin to blister. Lay tortillas out on a

(continued)

flat work space. Add the lettuce mix and then the burgers, chile side down. Fold the tortilla around the burger
and serve. *Serves 4*

Standing Firm on Burger Principles

i t is customary—if such a term can be applied to the famously mutable burger—that when local cooks trans-
form the American standard, they do so by way of toppings,
techniques, garnishes, and, to a lesser extent, substitutions.
Think burgers slathered with pimento cheese, burgers steamed
in steel boxes, and burgers cut with soy meal or onions. None
violate the bun-and-patty precepts we Americans hold to be
self-evident.

Rarely—very rarely—do you find cooks who tinker with the
basic form of the patty. Even when the folks at Matt's Bar in
Minneapolis stuff theirs with cheese, the result is still a patty.
There are, however, exceptions. In the chapter that follows,
I detail the loosemeats phenomenon, which has reached its
apogee in Iowa. By my lights and my palate, loosemeat sandwiches are different enough from sloppy joes—and similar

enough to the traditional patty form—to qualify as burgers, albeit deconstructed ones.

Just so you know, I don't imprudently embrace sandwiches that have no business being called burgers. I have my limits. I'm thinking of a cookbook that I read recently, one that advocates crafting patties of cranberries and ground chuck, rolling them in powdered hot chocolate mix, and serving the griddled choc-o-pucks between slices of sourdough. By my lights, that's not a burger. That's what happens when a rail car loaded with beef collides with a rail car loaded with berries, and a scavenging pastry chef makes dinner from the detritus.

NINE

Beef on the Loose

don Taylor Short was twenty-four when a friend of his grandfather's took him to a Rotary Club luncheon in Marshalltown, Iowa. The year was 1985. Short was nervous. He knew they were talking about him. Rumors had circulated for weeks about the insurgent youngster the Taylor family had pegged to take over their Maid-Rite. Everyone wanted to check him out.

Short wasn't a stranger to them. His great-grandfather, Clifford Taylor, was a Maid-Rite pioneer, the third man to open a franchise back in 1928. Clifford Taylor had been a friend of company founder Floyd Angell, and that went a long way with the locals.

Short's grandfather and namesake, Don Taylor, had also earned the respect and patronage of Marshalltown. At a time when many considered ground beef to be suspect, he put all questions about quality to rest when he installed a cooler in the basement and began grinding his own beef from Iowa steers. At his wedge-shaped stand, around his horseshoe counter, this close-knit river town defined itself, one sandwich at a time.

But family lineage is not always predictive. That's what the old folks said. Just as the Rotary lunch was served, a courtly gentleman, a friend of Don Taylor's, leaned in Short's ear and whispered, "Young man, don't you fuck with our Maid-Rite."

Short appears to be a little embarrassed by the story—he tugs at his necktie, adjusts his apron. But he admits the old man's admonition had resonance. "I listened to him," says Don. "It was like he was talking for the whole town."

Expand the area of influence to the entirety of Iowa—as well as contiguous states—and you'll get an idea of the true reach of those words. Based upon my travels, it's clear that these citizens of the prairies are deeply invested in their Maid-Rites. Problem is, they can't agree on what constitutes a Maid-Rite.

The next day, I meet with Bradley Burt, CEO of the Maid-Rite Corporation in Des Moines. He knows that a Maid-Rite is the trademark sandwich of his lockstep franchisees, doled out by "ambassadors of hospitality" who serve Maid-Rite and Cheese-Rite and Mega-Rite sandwiches, garnished with a "dose of nice." Burt tells me that, by standardizing procedures and portion control, he plans a "resurrection" of what he believes to be a moribund brand.

But after a couple more days on the road, I come to think he's got a fight on his hands. I stop at six Maid-Rites and meet four owner-operators. They don't speak of franchise dictates and system-wide standards, but of hometown philosophies shared by a confederation of owners. They mock the idea of an omnipotent home office like drunken salesmen in a David Mamet play.

From what I can glean, the seeds of resistance to Maid-Rite uniformity were sown in the days of Angell, who some historians say was the first American restaurant franchiser. He was an old-school haggler who sold some franchises for a dollar and a promise that the owner-operator buy a proprietary spice mix through a central commissary. He cinched other deals on a handshake, an agreement to buy paper cups and napkins from the home office, and a pledge to serve sandwiches garnished with nothing but mustard, onions, and pickles. In other words, Angell may well have codified the Maid-Rite sandwich. But he didn't manage to codify the business. He may not have even tried.

Perhaps he was a genius. After all, since Angell first claimed the trademark back in the 1920s, Maid-Rite—like Xerox and Kleenex—has come close to being accepted as a generic term for a crumbly sandwich of ground beef, embellished with chopped onions, sliced pickles, and yellow mustard, and served on a squishy hamburger bun. Like the Hamburg steak of yore, it's a lingua franca coinage recognized by disparate devotees.

But it strikes me that what Maid-Rite really has going for it isn't name recognition but an ability to cleave to hometown individuality while taking advantage of economies of scale. What's more, there's a certain retrograde appeal to these backsliding franchises, wherein a lapsed Baptist or a onetime Tender Foot might recognize something of their fraternal selves.

two more days of crisscrossing the state follow, during which my ideas about Maid-Rite's dominance of the genre are called into question, flounder, and then fall apart. The first sign of trouble comes at the Canteen, a back-alley Ottumwa, Iowa, institution. I know that crumbly burgers are served all over Iowa, not just at Maid-Rite franchises. But when I ask for a Maid-Rite, figuring that's what all crumbly burgers are called, the lady at the steamer—the one who is using what appears to be a cement trowel to stir the meat—says, without looking up, "If you want to order a sandwich, try asking for a canteen; that's what we serve."

Turns out that the people of Ottumwa have been cooking up sandwiches of pebbly ground beef since 1927. Like my friend Don Taylor Short, they eat theirs with nothing but a shake of salt, a squeeze of mustard, sliced pickles, and chopped onions. They began making them about the same time as Maid-Rite, but consider canteen sandwiches distinct.

Nomenclature is an issue all over what I've come to think of as the "loosemeats" belt. On Iowa's western extreme, in and around Sioux City, that's what they call a Maid-Rite. More

accurately, that's what they call a Maid-Rite if they're not patrons of Miles Inn, where a "Charlie boy" is the thing; or the
Tastee Inn & Out, where you ask for a "tastee"; or the late and
much lamented Ye Ole Tavern Inn—where, when you ordered a "tavern," your sandwich came with a spoon to scoop
up the loosemeats.

Loosemeats matter out west. One Sioux City native, Joye
Cook-Levy, went so far as to write a play, *Onion Girl*, which re-
volves around life at the Tastee Inn & Out. Action at the joint
proved to be compelling enough to snag Cook-Levy a slot
at the 2004 New York International Fringe Festival and a couple of encouraging reviews. (But in unguarded moments,
even some natives of Sioux City allow that loosemeats is a win-
cer of a word, reminiscent of the accurate but somehow im-
polite nutmeats, a term best left to candy makers.)

More contrary evidence awaits in Newton, back toward
the center of Iowa. I come across two diners serving almost
identical sandwiches. The buildings are mirror-image brick
rectangles, separated by a blacktop parking lot. Each has a
horseshoe-shaped counter. Each employs a cook who stuffs
pebbly burger meat into whitebread buns.

The joint on the left is the Snook Inn and calls its sandwiches beef burgers. Across the parking lot, the local Maid-Rite
outlet serves what appears to be the same darn food. But they
call their diminutive house special a "Joey-Rite." When I ask
why, I get a smile and a tongue-in-cheek story about a former
owner named Joey. Oh, Mr. Burt, I fear they will remember
you as a Sisyphus of franchised loosemeats, always battling
the incline.

never make it back to Des Moines, to Maid-Rite head-
quarters. Nor do I have a chance to explore the outer ter-
ritories, like Detroit, Michigan, where Lafayette Coney Island
serves loose burgers on hot dog buns, or Wichita, Kansas,
where the Nu Way Café serves its versions of Maid-Rites with
mugs of root beer. And I've come at the wrong time of year to
take in the Minnesota State Fair, where reliable sources tell
me that midway vendors peddle gizmo sandwiches of crumbled Italian sausage and ground beef.

But I do make it back to Marshalltown. From my perch at
Taylor's Maid-Rite, I watch the cook dig deep into a chest-
high stainless steel trough that looks something like an ar-
mored flower box. She chops and flips, chops and flips, as a
scree of ground beef arcs through the air and tendrils of
steam trace their way ceilingward. My sandwich is as good as
any I've eaten—satisfying and meaty in a primal sort of way,
but at the same time somehow cleaner, purer, more elemental. As I spoon the last errant bits of onion and beef into my
mouth, Don Taylor Short grabs a stool alongside.

I tell him what I've seen and heard and eaten, and of how
I've embraced the virtues of backsliding franchises. I tell him
that I've come to think of Iowa as a place where an eater can
understand that while the great majority of our milk is now
homogenized, our country isn't. Short smiles and tells me
about the pressure he's getting from Burt to use commissary-
issued, vapor-locked bags of seasoned and cooked beef. Burt
says it's a matter of establishing consistency across the brand.

When I ask Short whether he's going to capitulate, he leads me down the stairs to a basement freezer where a dozen or so front quarters of Iowa beef hang. "This one came from a county fair; it was raised up by some teenager out in the country," he says as he inspects a steer flank. "We don't have any need for bags of beef. We grind our own every morning." Then Short pauses. And he looks me in the eye and says, "I do believe this is just the kind of thing my grandfather's friend was talking about."

Deconstructed Iowa Burgers

The undated cookbook Recipes from Famous People and Bohemian Iowa Cookery, *compiled by the St. Elizabeth and St. Helena Circles of Sacred Heart Church in Oxford Junction, Iowa, includes four recipes for Maid-Rite style burgers. Along with various methods of spelling, the recipes dictate a wide variety of ingredients. But there are commonalities. Mrs. Mary Brinkman and Mrs. Don Brunscheen call for cans of chicken gumbo soup. I scratch my head over that for a good long while. And then I pick up a copy of a cookbook from the First Presbyterian Church of Algona, Iowa. Chicken gumbo again.*

I'm not going to go there. But I do understand the want for more than mere salt. This recipe straddles the line between the simplicity of Marshalltown Maid-Rites and the racy ideas promulgated by Iowa church ladies.

- 1 pound ground chuck
- 1 teaspoon ground pepper
- 1 teaspoon sugar
- 2 teaspoons dry mustard
- 1 teaspoon salt
- ½ cup water

- 6 buns
- Yellow mustard, to taste
- Dill pickles, sliced
- Medium onion, chopped

Place water in the bottom of a double boiler and bring to a boil, being careful not to let the water touch the top section of the boiler. Combine ground beef, pepper, sugar, mustard, and salt in the top of the double boiler. Cook, stirring all the while, until the meat is firm and pebbly and no longer pink. Add ½ cup of water. Reduce the heat and simmer for fifteen minutes, stirring occasionally, until the liquid in the mixture has nearly evaporated. Cover the meat.

(continued)

Slather buns with mustard. Add a couple of pickle slices. Use a slotted spoon to stuff the buns with the beef, pressing the beef into a semblance of a mound. Toss in a handful of chopped onions. Clamp the top bun down and serve with a coffee spoon. *Serves 6*

Greeks at the Flattop

many are the immigrants who have tried their hand at the burger business. Pakistani nationals long ran the Royal Burgers of Salt Lake City, dishing pastrami-and-beef-patty–stuffed buns. In New Orleans, a family of Croatian immigrants griddles the city's best onion burger at a suburban oyster house called Bozo's. But Greeks are the once and future kings of immigrant-peddled burgers.

Iggy Patsalis of Tomasita's in Santa Fe is a Greek standard-bearer. So was the late Prometheus Koustoubardis, who built a reputation in Dallas for dusting his Burger House burgers—and his fries and anything else that happened to be lying about his kitchen—with a raspy mix of salt and cumin.

In Los Angeles, Tommy Koulax, the son of Greek immigrants, made good on the sign that flashed above his Beverly Avenue location, Tommy's Original World Famous Hamburgers. In Chicago, the Billy Goat Tavern remains a Greek stronghold, immortalized by John Belushi in the Olympia Diner skits he did for *Saturday Night Live,* and by *Chicago Tribune* columnist Mike Royko. The latter declared the subterranean bunker to be one of the few places on earth where "a hamburger is still a hambooger and a cheeseburger is still a chizbooger."

And yet while the Greeks have gotten all the press, there are other ethnic groups who have contributed their own flair. Take the Cuban immigrants of Miami.

TEN

Fidel's Fritas

i begin my explorations along Eighth Street, known among
Miami's six-hundred-fifty-thousand strong Cuban popu-
lation as Calle Ocho. South and west of downtown, Calle
Ocho remains—more than forty-five years after Castro dis-
placed Batista and spurred the first flight for the Florida shore,
more than twenty years after the Mariel boatlifts brought a
new generation of Cubans to Miami—Little Havana's main
drag, a street carnival masquerading as a primary thorough-
fare. It's also ground zero for fritas, the Cuban riff on the
American standard.

Most exiles say fritas hearken to old Habana, where peddlers
sold buns stuffed with wafers of beef and piles of potato sticks
from kerosene-fueled carts. In Cuba, fritas were street food,

eaten on the go, in public. Natives of Havana now living in Miami recall the old men who rolled jerry-rigged hand trucks into place outside the city's baseball stadiums at the top of the ninth, to await the exiting hordes. And they remember the young boys who trundled bicycle-burros from distiller to manufacturer, from Plaza de Armas to Plaza de la Catedral, selling quick lunches for a few pesos.

O f course, I know none of this when I wander by El Rey de las Fritas (which translates loosely from the Spanish as The King of the Cuban Hamburgers). The morning is hot. I am skidding toward torpidity, in search of an apricot-flavored mamey milkshake to cool me down, when a hyperkinetic sign catches my eye.

I love the exuberance of the restaurant king's visage, the cheek-splitting grin, the red bow tie, the jade-encrusted crown. And so, though I am far from hungry, I duck inside and snag a seat at the counter, within sight of the grill, beneath a faux big top striped in seafoam green, fireplug red.

Mercedes Gonzales stands at the register, applying eyeliner with the aid of a mirror wedged into the cash drawer. She appears to be in her late twenties. And since the lunch rush is still an hour away, she's welcoming, talkative, and patient.

I try out my feeble Spanish. I'm not quite sure what I actually communicate, aside from curiosity, but my intent is to order a mamey milkshake—and a frita. Mercedes responds, in English, with a history lesson. She tells me that at the age of twelve, while still living in Havana, her father began working one of his brother's two frita carts. He made good money, she says. He was not a rich man, but his prospects were bright.

Soon he bought his own cart and began growing his own business, which he called something like El Capotolio. And then came Castro, in 1959. By 1960, most foreign-owned businesses had been nationalized. And during the Great Revolutionary Offensive of 1968, Castro nationalized more than fifty-five thousand Cuban-owned businesses and banned self-employment.

Mercedes's father fled the country, bound for Spain, where he worked odd jobs—baking macaroons, filing keys, cobbling shoes—before settling in Miami. "He was tough," Mercedes tells me. "He could pull money from the ground. But he did not forget his home. When he came to America, he brought Cuba with him; he brought fritas."

m y frita arrives on a particleboard platter. The bun cants open, overstuffed with splinters of potato and shreds of onion, trailing rivulets of brick-red sauce. I bite, and I learn that somewhere beneath these strata lies a ground beef patty, spiked with what tastes like paprika, maybe cumin, maybe oregano.

The bun is soft, yet slightly pliant, reminiscent of the flautas baked for the best Cubano sandwiches. But the fresh-fried potatoes win my devotion. They are shatteringly crisp, in the manner of those potato sticks sold by the can in convenience stores. Unlike those tinned goods, these potatoes are still warm from the oil; they still suggest the dank earth from which they were harvested.

Biting down through a nest of these potatoes, crunching through the stray onion, finding purchase in the thin patty of ground beef, I savor a burger as texturally complex, as sensually compelling as any that has ever crossed my palate.

i n America, burgers are largely apolitical. Neither Democrat nor Republican, they serve as proxies for our ideals, for our valorization of mobility, for our dedication to entrepreneurship.

There are exceptions: By way of worldwide ubiquity, burgers are sometimes depicted as exemplars of American hegemony. (Slow Food, a sociopolitical movement, has its origins in response to the opening of a McDonald's on Rome's ancient Piazza di Spagna.) And of late, catalyzed by Morgan Spurlock's film *Super Size Me,* McDonald's has proved a fulcrum for discussions of government-mandated nutritional reform. Of course, burgers can be targets of political groups—as in the failed PETA initiative of 2003, wherein the animal rights group offered Hamburg, New York, officials $15,000 worth of non-meat patties to change the city's name to Veggieburg.

u sually, burgers promise a break from matters of import, a diversion, accompanied by a heaping basket of fries. Miami confounds the paradigm. Here, as Mercedes would have it, burgers and politics are wed. Not to mention burgers and fries. Here, talk of burgers evokes discussions of political upheaval, of the struggle between good and evil, of capitalism versus communism.

Here, burgers—specifically fritas—link the onetime capitalism of Cubans living in Havana with the present-day capitalism of Cubans living in Miami. They are symbols of what was lost in the move to America, and what was soon regained. I find evidence everywhere—in the stacks and on the streets.

In the collections of the Miami public library, I come upon two newspaper clippings:

> In August of 1959, just one month after Castro nationalized U.S. businesses, Edwin Thompson of Pittsfield, Massachusetts, told his hometown paper that old Cuba and new coexisted. "Many of Castro's soldiers are still walking in the streets with handguns and rifles," he said. "But after you are here a few hours, you don't seem to notice them. They seem to be as much a part of the way of life in Cuba today as corner vendors cooking fritas." —*Berkshire Eagle*, August 6, 1959

> Five years hence, entrepreneurial activity was banished in Havana, and the fritas of Miami had come to symbolize the adaptation and ascendance of newly-arrived émigrés. "Cubans are in a score of industries, and what many of them contribute is far from menial," wrote syndicated columnist John Chamberlain in a special report from Miami. "They are in

fruit and vegetable canning, they operate garages, they own laundries, they have become canny used car salesmen, they add the authentic Latin note to night clubs, [and] they challenge the hamburger cult with little joints that sell delicious fritas." —*Chronicle-Telegram,* March 5, 1964

The next day, I visit two more frita stands. The first, Dago's Fritas Dominos, is plastered with newspaper clippings that document founder Ramón Estevil's flight from Cuba in 1962 and his subsequent stab at American-style commerce by means of a frita shop, inspired by El Sebastian, his favorite, the one he patronized in Cuba.

The second, El Mago (the magician) de las Fritas, offers much the same storyline: flight, rebound, triumph—all by means of burgers, of fritas. I order one. The El Mago frita has the bite of something like chorizo, and potatoes that crackle beneath my incisors.

Some claim that true fritas owe nothing to the burgers of America, that they are actually derivative of picadillo, the dish of spiced ground beef, nuts, and raisins long popular in Cuba. They will tell you that the original fritas were not patties but were loose in consistency—like south-of-the-border loosemeats—and were served in cones made from twisted tissue paper.

And they may be right. But the Cuban natives I met on the streets of Calle Ocho, not to mention their sons and daughters, were quick to claim some sort of American derivation. And they were just as quick to tell me that, although the sire of the frita may be American, its soul is Cuban.

I'll take that logic one step further. I'll say that fritas are the only offshore hamburgers—since the original German imports—that manage to claim dual citizenship. Burgers served on English muffins confuse the Brits. Roquefort smeared on patties of American Angus insults the French. But fritas are different. Divined in Havana, refined in Miami, propelled by forces both sociopolitical and gastronomical, they are symbol and sustenance, American and Cuban.

Fritas de Calle Ocho

Fried potatoes are all important here. And, as opposed to other sandwiches—say chip butties served at fish shops in and around Liverpool, England, or fry-stuffed and gravy-drenched poor boys served in New Orleans barrooms—they are included for texture, not as filler. So pull out that bottle of peanut oil; give yourself another ten minutes. Sure, you could reach for a can of those prefab potato sticks, but how are you going to look Mercedes in the eye when you finally make it down to Miami?

FOR THE FRITAS

- 1 cup vegetable or peanut oil
- 1 potato, sliced into thin matchsticks
- 1 teaspoon salt

In a heavy skillet, heat oil over a medium-high flame. Add the potatoes, stirring to distribute, and cook for 2 or 3 minutes until they are crisp, like chips. Seine from grease, salt generously, and set aside.

FOR THE BURGERS

- ½ cup bread crumbs
- ½ cup milk
- 1 pound ground round or chuck
- ¼ pound ground chorizo sausage *(you can use links, too, snipping the casings and crumbling the meat)*
- 1 onion, finely chopped
- 1 egg
- 2 cloves garlic, chopped
- 2 teaspoons tomato paste
- 1 teaspoon salt
- 1 teaspoon ground black pepper
- 1 teaspoon paprika
- American cheese

(continued)

- 8 buns
- Chili sauce
- Ketchup

Combine the bread crumbs and milk in a bowl. In a separate bowl, combine beef, chorizo, half of the onions, egg, garlic, and tomato paste. Sprinkle salt, paprika, and pepper. Drain the bread crumbs and add them, too.

Form the mixture into 8 patties, a little less than a half-inch thick. (To press them flat, try sandwiching patties between sheets of waxed paper and pressing down with a spatula.) Lightly oil a skillet set over medium-high heat and cook burgers for 2 to 4 minutes per side, flipping once and adding a slice of cheese to each as the burgers finish.

Toast buns and spread both sides with a mixture of one-half chili sauce, one-half ketchup. Scatter bun heels with remaining onions. Add cheese-draped patties and press matchstick potatoes into the cheese. Press crown bun on top and serve with more matchsticks. *Serves 8*

Ollie the Grouch

O llie Gleichenhaus cussed anyone who poured ketchup on his burger. And if you liked your meat cooked past medium, he would point toward a handwritten sign, tacked behind the register: "If you order my Ollie burger well-done, I suggest you order the hot dog instead."

Ask him what spice mix he used and he'd proclaim—arms flailing, sweat cascading from beneath his porkpie hat and down his wide brow—that ashes from his cigars were the secret. If you dared voice displeasure with a dish he served, Gleichenhaus would shut off the grill, lower the blinds, and escort every last customer out the door. If he didn't like you, he might retire a spent Monte Cristo on your plate. (If he liked you, he might halo your nose in smoke rings.)

In 1971, Gleichenhaus was sixty-one, a thirty-six-year veteran of Ollie's, a Miami Beach sandwich shop at the corner of Collins Avenue and Twenty-third Street. In addition to a talent for invective, he possessed an everyman's élan that appealed to hipsters and pensioners and tourists alike. He was a local celebrity, a cantankerous and colorful exemplar of a peculiar American type: the ill-tempered grill cook with a mustard-splattered apron and a well-concealed heart of gold. Plus, his burgers were delicious.

———

One fall, John Y. Brown, the Kentucky businessman-cum-politician who made Colonel Sanders a household name and a very rich man, grabbed a booth at Ollie's. The buzz on Gleichenhaus's way with burgers was building. And Brown was on the prowl for a new business venture.

Brown ate five burgers in one sitting. When Gleichenhaus emerged from the kitchen to find out who the man with the appetite was, Brown praised his burger and proposed to build a new fast food business around the old man. In the process, Brown would make Gleichenhaus a colonel, too. "We ain't going to do nothing," Gleichenhaus snarled, "unless you make me a five-star general."

After a bit of negotiation, Brown bought Gleichenhaus's burger recipe, the one with twenty-three herbs and spices. (According to *The New York Times*, the tab was a cool million.) Soon, Gleichenhaus was the face and voice of a new chain of trolley-shaped walk-up stands called Ollie's Trolley. He cut radio ads, taped television commercials. He worked with a band of flavor chemists to standardize his trademark burger seasoning. He smiled for the cameras and planned his retirement.

The Ollieburger was a salty and musky riff on tradition, a burger that, if my memory of the suburban Atlanta Ollie's Trolley of the early 1970s serves, tasted vaguely of Mediterranean climes: Think of oregano-spiked burgers as served at Greek diners across the country, but perhaps most memorably at Alex's Tavern in Memphis. Or of the cumin-laced burgers dished by the Burger House in Dallas. And then imagine a confluence of all. A burger that somehow tastes of a gone-to-seed Miami Beach, of salt and sand and sea. A burger that evokes a randy old man who chomps on cigars, cusses a blue streak, and appreciates the sinuous lines of the feminine physique. The Ollieburger tasted like that. Only more so.

b rown's timing was impeccable. Grouches like Gleichenhaus were in vogue. *All in the Family* debuted in January. That spring, thanks in large part to Carroll O'Connor's bravura performance as Archie Bunker, the series won the Emmy for outstanding comedy. In crotchety Gleichenhaus, Brown had tapped the Archie zeitgeist and found the persona around which he could build a brand.

But Brown blinked. Somewhere along the way, he and his suits denuded Gleichenhaus of his innate charm. They told him to clean up his language. They convinced him to embrace ketchup as a condiment. Gone were the Bermuda shorts and T-shirts of his Miami Beach days. In their place, he wore straw boaters, ascots, and knee-length aprons.

The heyday of Ollie's Trolleys was short-lived. By the fall of 1974, the prospects for hundreds of locations were dim; the chain consisted of just fifty-odd trolleys. And many of those were failing.

Problems were multifaceted. Some said Ollieburgers were too spicy for Middle America. Others said the dollar price tag was too high. Others still didn't warm to the trolleys, claiming that, in size and shape, they evoked grimy lunch wagons and greasy spoons—the very places, I might add, that gave birth to characters like Ollie Gleichenhaus.

T he story of Ollie Gleichenhaus is, at its core, the story of our nation's conflicted love affair with the burger: The Ollieburger was born of hardscrabble America. Of proud working-class roots. It was aggressively seasoned. It was a gut punch of a dish. I imagine that the marketers who would make Gleichenhaus a star knew this. They probably also knew that while Americans might embrace his backstory, what would sell was a kinder and gentler Gleichenhaus, a milder and more universally palatable burger.

They likely recognized that Americans appreciate the hedonistic appeal of griddled cow flesh. They acknowledged that a burger calls to mind our primal selves. And they determined that, just as we weren't ready to take a peek into an abattoir where cow flesh became hamburger meat, just as we weren't likely to embrace a chain of restaurants that recalled the suspect diners of our not-too-distant past, we weren't ready to come face-to-face with an unvarnished Ollie Gleichenhaus. He was too raw, too real. And so were his burgers.

U ntil recently, I thought that the saga of Ollie Gleichenhaus would amount to nothing more than an historical footnote. I thought that all the Ollie's Trolleys had closed. Once in a while, I would come upon an old trolley, retrofitted as a cab stand or a locksmith's shop or a coffee shop. I figured that none of the restaurants had survived the seventies. Surely, none lived on after Gleichenhaus himself died in 1991.

But while in Louisville, Kentucky, I happened upon a red-and-yellow Ollie's Trolley, poised on a brick base at the corner of Third and Kentucky streets. The trappings of old were there: A faded sign by the door of the trolley proclaimed the Ollieburger to be the "ultimate achievement in hamburgery." Another advertisement, a message from the man himself, proclaimed, "It took me 40 years to perfect my Ollieburger, searching for just the right seasonings, sauce, and a way to seal in the juices and flavor. . . . My goal in life is to share with you the fruits of my work."

The burger tasted like it should. Of cumin and oregano. Of salt. And although the grill cook was cheerful and young and black instead of cantankerous and old and white, he struck me as a worthy inheritor of the Ollie legacy. It turned out, however, that he is not the sole contender for that crown. Two months later, I discovered another Ollie's in Washington, D.C.

This was not a trolley but a bricks-and-mortar restaurant, moored on the ground floor of a hotel. It had, over the course of thirty years of unregulated operation, gone native. Somewhere along the way, the proprietors opened a patio and dubbed it Ollie's Oasis. What's more, they began turning out a rendition of the Ollieburger that was a tad sweeter than the norm. (Perhaps, like Swenson's of Akron, Ohio, they add sugar to the mix.) And they bolstered the menu with dishes Gleichenhaus never offered, like crab cakes and the locally famed sausages known as half-smokes.

Still more Ollieburgers loom on my horizon. Sources in Cincinnati tell me that an entrepreneur named Marvin Smith—who has been known to wear a yellow bandana around his neck and a tufted chef's toque on his head—has plans to revitalize the chain. After toiling in obscurity for ten years, his prospects brightened in 2003 when two local restaurant critics posted rave reviews of Smith's original trolley in the city's West End neighborhood. One reviewer, however, singled out Smith's rib rips and black-eyed peas instead of his burgers.

Sales boomed. By early that spring, Smith opened a second location. And in the fall of 2004, he opened a third, across the river in Covington, Kentucky. "I want to be the next Colonel Sanders," he told a reporter. "I want to be the guy in a chef's hat who gets paid lots of money to travel around to the new Ollie's Trolley restaurants." With any luck, Smith will make general by the time you hold this book in your hands.

on
the
fringes

ELEVEN

Deep-Fried Memphis

i am haunted by an image from the evening news. I saw it in the early nineties, but it still plays in my head like a dream. I remember the scene this way:

I'm sitting on the edge of a bed in a Memphis hotel room, clicking through TV channels, when sirens blare from the box. I watch three motorcycle cops in wraparound shades breach rush-hour traffic, escorting a vat of grease through the streets. A pompadoured reporter steps in front of the camera to explain:

"Dyer's Hamburgers, a Memphis institution since 1912, is moving to a new Cleveland Avenue location. Inside, the orange booths sparkle, the tile floor gleams. The only thing that isn't new at Dyer's is the grease in which the burgers fry. The owners claim that they never change out the grease, and that is the secret to their success. Deputy Sheriff Billy Barlow, a longtime customer who was weaned on Double-Doubles, is in charge of the security detail for the relocation effort."

An interview with Barlow follows. Then the camera cuts to a burbling cauldron of vintage grease and zooms in, framing a burger as it bobs in the muck like a dinghy at sea.

three years pass before I get my first taste. In the interim, I move from northern Georgia to northern Mississippi. The burger I covet is now a mere seventy miles away.

On a spring day, I drive north from Oxford. I'm not quite sure what I will find. I envision Dyer's as a lesser Waffle House, shrouded in an oily fog of tallow and tobacco. Or maybe it's a curbside shebang with a roof of corrugated tin. What I discover instead is a clean, spare storefront in a down-at-the-heels strip shopping center.

Behind the counter is proprietor Mark McKinn, a foppish blond with an anxious smile. He's a one-man show, jockeying between the register and a wok-shaped vat of that famous grease. I order a Double-Double, just like the deputy.

McKinn swings a wooden mallet with authority. The report—a concussive thwack that sounds like Friday night football, like helmet on shoulder pads—echoes through the room. What was a racquet ball–sized lump of ground beef is now a ragged web of pink. With the sides of his spatula, McKinn shapes the meat into a vague circle; pushes aside hot dogs and hamburgers already burbling in the cauldron of seasoned beef fat (otherwise known as tallow); slips the little disk in, and watches as it slides toward the bottom. One more thwack follows, one more disk.

Two minutes later, that first burger bobs to the surface. It's nut-brown in color, shading toward black at the periphery. McKinn scoops the meat from its berth, slaps a slice of cheese on top, and skims the combo back through the grease to melt the cheese. Piggybacking the second burger and the second slice, he weds the crown bun to the burger stack with his spatula before flipping the payload onto a heel bun already slathered with mustard and scattered with onions and pickles.

I eat, savoring the profoundly beefy flavor. The taste is pleasantly rank, in the manner of dry-aged beef teetering on the brink of perfection. I wish the cheese were better. And it would be nice if he toasted—or at least warmed—his buns, but those are minor quibbles. I pay my respects to McKinn, grab a menu for future reference, and exit with a promise to return.

nine more years pass, during which I make six or eight treks. McKinn usually meets me at the register. And the burgers are as beefy as I recall, as unapologetically greasy and undeniably good.

One day, I wander in during the late afternoon lull and, after dishing my Double-Double, McKinn slides into the booth opposite me and lays out the Dyer's story. He spins a good yarn, about how Elmer Dyer, a Mississippi boy, came to the big city in 1912 with a head full of ideas about how to cook a burger.

The upshot is this: Old man Dyer cooked his burgers in a deep skillet. In time, he noticed that they tasted best when fried in a shallow puddle of their own fat. (If you think this technique is gratuitously greasy, remember that duck confit is, by definition, duck preserved and then cooked in *its* own fat.) Over the years, that puddle got deeper, until Dyer was frying them in a deep reservoir of fat that he strained every night, retaining a measure of the previous day's effluvium, and storing it for the next batch in the manner that a baker of sourdough bread saves a starter.

On another visit, I ask McKinn about the television spectacle I witnessed. He confirms that the procession took place. But he shies away from claiming that the grease in which he cooks burgers is the very same stuff Elmer Dyer used. "Some of the same molecules are floating in the grease," he tells me. "They've got to be, but I won't tell you it's the exact same stuff."

Sometime in 2001, I stop by for a burger and find that, although the Cleveland Avenue Dyer's is still in business, it's now run by a Vietnamese family. They assure me that McKinn left the grease when he departed. I order spring rolls, hoping that they, too, will benefit from a dip in the hallowed tallow. But neither measure up; the savor is gone. (Six months later, I drive by and notice that the Dyer's sign is gone, too.)

Three years of wandering in the wilderness follow, during which I search for analogues. I taste slug burgers in Mississippi that get their distinctive crunch from an immersion in scalding oil. I eat burgers in Ohio that don't so much fry as poach in a mixture of oil and rendered tallow. I even visit a newfangled Dyer's on Beale Street in Memphis, but McKinn is nowhere to be found, and my burger lacks the bovine wallop his had.

Along the way, my search morphs—from a quest for a burger cooked in its own fat, to a burger that illustrates our conflicted responses to fat. To wit: We know that great burgers are usually predicated on beef with a fat quotient of 20 percent. We recognize that fat carries flavor. And yet we declaim our predilections as somehow unenlightened, our palates as atavistic.

for a short time, in 2003 and early 2004, I believe that the proper locus for my fat burger explorations is Tucker's Tavern, a cement-floored New Orleans barroom, located alongside LSU Medical Center and beneath the I-10 overpass. Owner Mike LaBorde stakes his reputation on stuffed burgers, gargantuas of the form, battered and then fried in 400-degree grease.

The frying in deep fat intrigues me. Over the course of a few visits, I work my way through the menu. I try the Big Al, chocked with pepperjack and mushrooms. I eat a good third of a Big Cajun, stuffed with bacon, sausage, mozzarella, and cheddar. With a friend, I split a Cordon Tuck, a burger stuffed with Swiss cheese, ham, and—you guessed it—a lobe of chicken breast. I even cadge the cook, Josh Shonts, in an unsuccessful attempt to taste his latest work in progress, a Benedict burger stuffed with Canadian bacon and a poached egg, served between Hollandaise-smeared English muffins.

Each dish arrives at table a sandy brown. The burgers are uniformly crunchy on the outside, juicy and flecked with onion and green pepper on the inside. And despite their berth in oil, they are, as LaBorde promised, no more grease-slicked than the norm.

But there are problems. I'm not sure these really qualify as burgers. They are more akin to punch lines, absurdist rejoinders to the critics who foretell a day when all sustenance will be delivered in burger form. And they are fried in peanut oil rather than tallow. According to the gospel of Elmer Dyer, that's cheating.

In time, I give up on making sense of our conflicted responses to fat. I'm back to pining for a fat-enriched burger when, at the invitation of a friend, I gambol about Memphis on a burger-eating pilgrimage.

After we down a Greek-spiced burger at Alex's, a half-century-old beer joint with the best jukebox in town, disappointments mount quickly. Jesus Coney Island, home of the Jonah Jumbo Cheeseburger, is out of business. The Green Beatle, open since 1939 and famous for its chili-cheeseburgers, is closed. And the Gridiron, the strip mall hang where Elvis liked to eat Palm Beach burgers slathered with Mrs. Weaver's brand pimento cheese, is but a ghost of its former self.

Bradley's, in a low-rent shopping center out in the far eastern reaches of town, shows promise. Truth be told, it reminds me of the old Cleveland Avenue Dyer's. The smell is familiar. The same pall of grease in the air. Though the fries are gossamer—twice-cooked, well salted, and served in a metal bowl—I focus on the burgers, which are—lo and behold—cooked in a rectangular cauldron, burbling with grease.

The cook calls his method pan-broiling, but I know a Dyer's riff when I see it. I scarf my burger and pronounce myself sated. Sure, the beefy taste is lacking, but I'm tired of all this Sturm und Drang. That's when my friend suggests a visit to Dyer's.

I beg off, thinking she means the Beale Street pretender. But she's thinking of the Dyer's out on Summer Avenue. She says it's the true inheritor of the Cleveland Avenue tradition. As a winter squall bears down upon the city, we drive crosstown, bound for yet another down-at-the-heels storefront.

And there he is, behind the counter. Of course, Mark McKinn doesn't recognize me. I'm just one of the acolytes that stand before him every day. I order a burger. I listen for the telltale thwack. I smile. I polish off said burger in record time, relishing the richness, the marrowbone whang of the meat. And I begin pestering him anew about the grease.

I point out a newspaper clipping tacked to the wall wherein his grandfather admitted that the Dyer's claim to age-old grease is a marketing conceit. McKinn blinks. "Sure, the grease changes," he says. "We clean it, we strain it, and add to it. And we toss in onions and Worcestershire sauce every morning. But I'm sticking by the molecule theory."

Tallow-Poached Burgers

I recognize that many readers may blanch at the thought of carting home a bucket of tallow. And I'll concede that this is not a recipe you're likely to whip up once a fortnight. But the savor of burgers cooked in this fashion is well worth the trouble. They taste elemental. Atavistic even. And if you have any tallow left over, you can always thumb through the Whole Earth Catalog *for soap and candle recipes.*

- 1½ pounds ground round
- 1 onion, chopped
- 1 teaspoon salt
- 1 teaspoon pepper
- 1 tablespoon Worcestershire sauce
- Wax paper
- 8 ounces shortening
- 8 ounces beef tallow (*Tallow is rendered beef fat, which you can probably get through your butcher. If that is out of the question, substitute 8 or more ounces of shortening and add 1 teaspoon powdered beef bouillon*)
- 1 onion, sliced thin

- 5–10 buns
- 5–10 slices American cheese
- Yellow mustard
- Dill pickles, sliced

Combine the meat, chopped onions, salt, pepper, and Worcestershire sauce together in a bowl. Working on a sheath of wax paper, shape the beef into 10 round balls. Top with another layer of wax paper. With a heavy spatula or mallet, press the burgers as flat as you are able. Warm the buns in a low oven.

Meanwhile, in a cast-iron skillet set over medium-high heat, heat the shortening and tallow until they begin to burble. Add the sliced onions. When the mixture begins to burble again, slide the burgers in. Wait 3 or so minutes. When they bob to the top, slap a slice of cheese on, spread the buns with the condiments, and serve. *Makes 10 burgers; you may want (to serve them as) doubles*

Beauty and the Bun

a s we wandered about Memphis, my friend began to fixate upon the quality of the buns, like a latter-day Goldilocks. Some, she said, were cold. Some were stale. Most were too small to support their payload. Although a couple were nicely toasted, none of the Memphis buns really pleased her.

A few days later, I came across this quote from Ray Kroc of McDonald's fame: "It requires a certain kind of mind to see beauty in a hamburger bun. Yet is it any more unusual to find grace in the texture and softly carved silhouette of a bun than to reflect lovingly on the hackles of a fishing fly? Or the arrangements and textures on a butterfly's wing?"

Kroc got me to thinking. About the chewy, salt-flecked pretzel bun I tore through at Rockenwagner's in Santa Monica. About the firm Italian rolls that Solly's Grille in suburban Milwaukee offers as an option on its butter burgers. About the loaves of crisp Leidenheimer's French bread on which they serve onion burgers at Bozo's in suburban New Orleans. About the magic lid theory of the transcendental bun, advanced by Ron Baber of Ron's Hamburgers and Chili in Tulsa, wherein the optimal ratio of cushy to crusty is achieved by covering buns with a metal salad bowl lid while they concurrently steam and crisp on the flattop.

And, of course, about the Portuguese buns—and rice-based bun proxies—of Hawaii.

TWELVE

Do the Loco Moco

I had the answer, and the answer was loco moco.

Typically, surveys of American gastronomy neglect Hawaii. Never mind that this lovely archipelago became a U.S. Territory in 1900 and has been a state since 1959. Never mind the bullet they took for us all at Pearl Harbor. Too often, we dismiss the food culture of our southernmost state as too confounding. Poi? Spam Musubi? They just don't translate. So goes the argument.

I would be different. I would make an incontrovertible case that loco moco—the beloved Hawaiian dish of rice, topped with a ground beef patty, crowned with an over-easy egg, and drenched in brown gravy—deserves a place in the canon of American burgers. I would argue that the glutinous rice at

the base of a loco moco serves as proxy for a bun. I would de-
fend the presence of an egg by citing similar practices at state-
side burger bellwethers like Tobacco Road in Miami and the
White Spot in Charlottesville, Virginia. I would rationalize
that gravy is nothing but brown ketchup.

At the time I came to these conclusions, I had not yet set
foot in Hawaii. But I'd read enough to know that the late
Richard Inoyue, founder of the Lincoln Café in Hilo, likely
invented the dish in 1949. And I knew that a group of
teenagers who called the café home came up with the name,
conjoining loco (Hawaiian pidgin for crazy) with moco (a
nonsensical but melodic bookend).

On my flight from the mainland, I compiled a list of loco
moco purveyors and perused the available scholarship, including volume thirty of the journal *Social Processes in Hawaii*, which
includes James Kelly's linguistic deconstruction, "Loco Moco:
A Folk Dish in the Making." And I checked off my prep work:
I had Rachel Laudan's book *The Food of Paradise* in my bag
and the number of Joan Namkoong, onetime food editor of
the *Honolulu Advertiser*, programmed into my cell phone.

d riving in from the Honolulu airport, I swing my rental
into Sam Choy's, a warehouse restaurant decorated
like a Polynesian Red Lobster. Loco moco dishes make up
their own section of the menu. In addition to Da Hilo Original, I have my choice of Da Pake (with Chinese lup cheong
sausage), Kalua Pork (with shredded, pit-cooked butt meat),
as well as vegetarian and fish options.

I order an original, with a side of Tater Tots. The first dish arrives in a widemouthed bowl, aswim in soy and beef gravy. The second comes sprinkled with green onions and drenched in a sweet-and-sour sauce of the kind you regularly find at small-town Chinese buffeterias. Each dish is good—in its own way. But I'm hard pressed to divine a burger—much less locate a patty—betwixt the egg and the rice, amongst all the gravy. Yet I am not disillusioned; I am challenged. I pledge to open my eyes to this new paradigm. In time, I will see the tree in the forest.

a t breakfast the next morning, Joan, a forty-something-year-old who wears her black hair in a bob and favors Grace Kelly sunglasses, tries to save me from myself. She has written a couple of books on local foods; Joan knows her stuff, knows Hawaii's food history. She also knows my type—blockheaded, determined to argue my own theory. But Joan is patient. Joan makes time for everyone. Even blockheads like me.

When I tell her I am researching a book on hamburgers in America and am interested in exploring the loco moco phenomenon, she deflects my query and gently steers the conversation back to what she calls "local burgers." Have you tried a local burger? she asks. I don't think to inquire about what defines a local burger; I tell her I'll get around to it, just as soon as I eat my fill of loco moco.

That afternoon, I join her on a walk through Chinatown. We ogle green frogs and red turtles and all manner of ungainly sea creatures like geoducks. We sample dragon fruit and rambutan. At a cubbyhole bakery, we nibble on crystallized ginger that steals my breath and angel food cake that lives up to its name.

Of course, I steer our conversation back to loco moco. I tell her about the trip I've planned to the Big Island, to the town of Hilo where it all began. "You can get great local burgers on the Big Island," she tells me. "That's where our beef industry began, where the British introduced cows to Hawaii in the late 1700s.

"Vancouver was the British captain who brought Texas longhorns to King Kamehameha," she continues. "He got the king to promise that cattle would be taboo for ten years, until they had time to multiply. By that time, the cows were pests and Kamehameha was bringing in Vaqueros to hunt feral cattle on horseback."

As Joan talks, my mind drifts. I summon the crescent bay around which Hilo sprawls, the craggy volcanoes towering above. In my mind's eye, I see orchid bogs, wiliwili thickets. On my mind's palate, I taste free-range loco moco.

C afé 100, a boomerang-roofed Hilo walk-up, is the place many consider the inheritor of the Lincoln Café tradition. A backlit menu board proclaims the members of the Loco Moco Family. Their clan is evidently legion: Burger locos, sure, but also Spam locos and Little Smokies sausage locos, too; mahimahi locos and oyako locos; bacon locos, chili locos, and beef stew locos. Of course, children can order Loco Moco

Magic Meals. And all plates come with a packet of Heinz and a matching packet of Kikkoman.

But I can't handle Café 100. I'm so flummoxed by the plethora of choices—not to mention alternately enchanted and repulsed by the wall-mounted superhero with a mighty SL (for Super Loco Moco Man) tattooed on his chest, charging forward to do battle with the forces of evil while balancing a three-tiered loco moco platter on his upstretched left hand—that I freak. I'm a kid in a candy store with a pocketful of quarters. I'm a junkie with a refillable scrip for methadone. And then I'm gone.

I end up across town, at Koji's Bento, a street corner café with one table, operated by a gentleman of Japanese descent. "I'm local Japanese," he tells me. "I've never seen Japan." Koji serves all manner of loco mocos, including a supreme (two beef patties, one egg, and kimchee), a deluxe (one more patty, plus macaroni salad), and a Koji special, the most expensive loco moco, with two homestyle patties, two nubs of chaurice (sausage), and one egg, smothered in both teri sauce and beef gravy, with sides of kimchee and macaroni salad.

At first glance, the menu reads like a mishmash of cultural dissonances. Upon second glance I decide that the Koji special might comprise the ideal polyglot platter, the perfect evocation of the Japanese (teriyaki), Korean (kimchee), Portuguese (chaurice), and American (macaroni salad) immigrants who have come to claim Hawaii as their own.

I settle in. Despite open windows and strategically placed fans, the air inside is steamy. But Koji's doesn't smell greasy in the manner of many a short-order café. It smells good, like the interior of a casserole dish brimming with stewbeef and carrots. I scrutinize the menu further.

Why, I ask Koji, does a homestyle hamburger cost more than a hamburger? "It's different," he tells me. "It's a local burger."

A light goes on. Joan's words float through my head. I ditch my loco moco. And I order a homestyle hamburger. Koji obliges and, for good measure, slips a serving of kimchee between hand-formed patty and the sweet Portuguese bun.

I chomp down, through the soft caress of the roll and the pickled cabbage, and into the meatloaf-like patty of beef. I know in that moment that I have found my mark. And I'm soon wondering what else I have overlooked.

t he next day, back in Honolulu, Joan joins me for the last lunch of my trip. We meet at the Diamondhead Market and Grill, a combination food bar and specialty grocer. While we wait for our burgers to arrive, I steal back to the counter and peer inside the kitchen. I hear a shuffle of feet behind me and turn to find Joan—along with proprietor Kelvin Ro, decked in chef's whites.

Joan explains to him how I came to Hawaii in search of local takes on burgers. His face brightens. And she tells him about my loco moco obsession. His face dims. (Joan does not know that the veil has lifted, because I'm too embarrassed to tell her.) So when Kelvin offers to show me how he makes a local burger—how he mixes bread crumbs and onions and egg into the chuck, how he seasons them on the grill with a mix of turbinado sugar, rock salt, and black pepper—I shoot

Joan a look that says, *OK, he doesn't know squat about loco moco; but I'll humor him.*

Local Burger

The sugar in this burger links Hawaii with Ohio, which is the only other state in America where I've seen sugar pop up with regularity in patty mixes. In Ohio, it's likely the legacy of the Menches brothers who, in 1885, began adding sugar to beef when they ran out of pork to grill. Today, drive-ins like Swenson's in Akron still add a touch of sugar to their burgers. And so do some of the best grill cooks in Hawaii.

BURGERS

- 1 pound ground chuck
- 1 small onion, minced
- 1 egg, beaten
- ½ cup unseasoned bread crumbs
- 1 teaspoon salt (Kosher or other large-grain)
- 1 tablespoon pepper
- 1 tablespoon sugar (preferably raw and brown)
- 2 tablespoons soy sauce

(continued)

In a large bowl, mix all ingredients until combined. Form into 6 patties. Heat a charcoal grill to medium-high heat and cook burgers for 2 to 3 minutes per side.

HOMESTYLE TERI SAUCE

Teri sauce is far different from its Japanese antecedent. In Japan, teriyaki sauce is simply a combination of soy sauce and a sweet cooking wine called mirin. But Japanese plantation workers could not easily obtain mirin in Hawaii. Sugar was the natural substitute, argues Rachel Laudan in The Food of Paradise: Exploring Hawaii's Culinary Heritage. *And the ginger and green onions were likely Chinese additions.*

- 1 cup soy sauce
- ¼ cup sugar, preferably raw and brown
- ½ tablespoon fresh ginger, grated
- 1 clove garlic, minced
- ¼ cup green onion, minced
- ½ teaspoon Accent

Combine all ingredients in a small bowl and set aside.

ASSEMBLY

- Mayonnaise
- 6 crusty rolls *(Portuguese style rolls are preferred but can be difficult to find in some areas)*

- 1 onion, sliced
- ¼ head iceberg lettuce
- 1 tomato, sliced

Smear mayonnaise on top buns. Swab both sides of the burgers with thin coatings of teri sauce. Place patties on bottom buns, followed by onion, lettuce, and tomato. Cap with crown bun. *Serves 6*

That's No Hovel! That's a Landmark

ll burger roads lead to the sprawling metropolis of Los Angeles. Bob Wian, popularizer of the double-decker, sire of Bob's Big Boy, got his start out in Glendale. Lionel Sternberger, claimant of the cheeseburger, worked the grill over in Pasadena. And, of course, the brothers McDonald opened their first stand in San Bernardino.

As the city has grown, Angelenos have developed strong affections for their burger purveyors. The more devout have come to appreciate the life stories of the industry's titans. The true believers have begun to fight to save from the wrecking ball the old-line open-air walk-ups crafted, in the 1930s and 1940s, from cast-off aluminum, maybe surplus steel.

When developers wanted to tear down the Munch Box in Chatsworth and throw up an office building, local high-school students collected 1,500 signatures in protest. When the faithful patrons of Irv's Burgers of West Hollywood learned their favorite joint might be replaced by a corporate coffee shop, they wrote protest letters, circulated petitions, and formed a self-styled Burger Brigade.

Most famously, when, in 2000, a property owner threatened the beloved Jay's Jayburgers of Silver Lake with an astronomical rent hike, the city pitched a two-week collective hissy fit that drew the attention of two buyers with an appreciation for hamburger vernacular, architecture, and comparatively deep pockets.

THIRTEEN

Going for Baroque

i have six LA burgers under my belt when I claim a seat at
Jay's Jayburgers, a four-stool metal hut, set hard alongside
Santa Monica Boulevard. The passenger seat of my rental car is
covered with menus, the floorboard littered with spent paper
cups and crumpled, logo-blazoned bags. In-N-Out, Cassell's,
Mo' Better Meatty Meat Burgers, Fat Burger, Apple Pan, and
Tommy's Original are in my rearview mirror. Tom's #5, Master
Burger, Chronis' Famous Sandwich Shop, and a little spot set in
a derelict bowling alley are just a few of the stars on the horizon.

At Jay's I sit with my back to the traffic, beneath a sawtooth
awning, eyeing the grill cook as he works. Burger construction,
as practiced in Los Angeles, is an exacting enterprise. In this
car-focused culture where meals are consumed on the go, between gearshifts and cell phone bleats, it's important to build

a burger with enough structural integrity to retain its burger-ness, even during a seventy-five-mile-an-hour lunch meeting on the 405. The grill cook at Jay's knows this cold.

He trowels a spoonful of cumin-scented chili onto the bottom bun in the same manner a mason applies grout to brick; drapes a slice of cheddar across a double-decker of half-inch patties so that the cheese binds one layer of beef to the next; toasts the top bun to ensure that, even upon prolonged contact with a sheath of lettuce, the bread will not turn to mush; and wraps the burger in a paper envelope designed to contain errant globs of condiment. It seems as though he does all of these things at the same time. Every effort—every ingredient—is employed with a kind of architectural intent that yields a burger of eminent portability.

C ontrary to the image broadcast by glam chefs and X-ray starlets, this sprawling city is not the province of *cuisine minceur.* Indeed, if you avoid Beverly Hills and pilot your car along one of LA's neon-washed, east-west thoroughfares—say Pico or Wilshire or Whittier Boulevard, roadways where you might glance at a forty-foot muffler man perched atop a garage or a blond figurehead fronting a beauty shop—you will come to know another city altogether. Here, in the real LA, burgers are king and pools of grease pop on flattop griddles. Here, stacks of buns await swabbing with the pickle relish–spiked sauce that outlanders have the temerity to call Thousand Island Dressing.

The early years of Los Angeles burger culture are not well documented. There are no genesis stories, no tales of the accidental flattening of a meatball to pass off as an epiphanic moment during which the local take on the burger was born. More than likely, Angelenos came to know and love burgers about the same time they came to know and love automobiles.

The traceable history of burgers in LA begins with the story of Ptomaine Tommy. His real name was Tommy DeForest, and from 1913 to 1958 he was the majordomo of local burgerdom. More than likely, DeForest, who claimed Mae West and Mary Pickford as regulars, was the restaurateur who popularized the ladling of a masa-thickened, beanless chili on a burger. Appreciated from a remove of more than a half century, DeForest's addition of chili may well have been the first step toward the baroque.

b aroque. Besides offering the promise of alliteration, that adjective best describes the prevailing burger ethic of Los Angeles. Singles topped by teetering hillocks of pastrami; double-puck hockey burgers crossed with hot dog "hockey sticks," and served between planks of Armenian flatbread; chili-slathered, cheese-capped disks of chuck, smothered by an omelet of eggs and chorizo, the whole affair trapped within two griddle-toasted buns: the burgers of Los Angeles defy notions of propriety. And they require, at a minimum, six napkins.

t oday, Los Angeles is rife with burger joints named Tom's or Tommy's or Big Tommy's. Some may descend from Ptomaine Tommy's, while others claim a lineage that dates back to a Greek immigrant named Tommy Koulax who, in a 1946 bid for differentiation, opened a burger stand that he dubbed Tommy's Original.

Typical of the genre, and perhaps a cut above many of the spots that share some version of that moniker, was Tom's #5, my next stop. The burgers served up at this bunker of a restaurant on Pico Boulevard were nothing fancy: thinish patties cooked on a flattop; smothered, upon request, in a torrent of chili and chopped onion.

But Tom's #5 also serves burgers topped with chorizo (a nod to Mexico, where the spicy sausage is favored), burgers topped with fried eggs (a tip of the hat to Uruguay and other South American countries where the practice of serving protein atop protein is commonplace), and burgers strewn with bell-shaped cascabel peppers, which, I would imagine, have their roots in the Cal-Mex taco stands of East LA. (For the record, I ate a burger dressed with a chorizo omelet. It was greasy-good food, especially when washed down with a cup of horchata, a cinnamon-flavored rice-water drink that proved to be the ideal antidote to heartburn.)

Four bites into my chorizo burger, I began to develop a theory, which gained strength during a subsequent stop at Master Burger in South LA—another typical outdoor stand with window service, trestle tables, and a roster of offerings that reads like a menu from the United Nations dining room. I passed on the Buffalo wings, the teriyaki beef plate, the ham torta, and, against my better judgment, the pastrami chili-cheese fries. Instead, I ordered a cheeseburger. But when it arrived, my burger looked so forlorn that I sent it back for modification. They sluiced the patty with chili; they piled on pastrami. And I succumbed.

But not before recognizing, in Master Burger, a sort of metaphor for multiethnic Los Angeles. I had noted similar influences at, say, Korean-owned Cassell's Hamburgers. But here was an over-the-top tribute to the myriad peoples who call this, the second largest city in the nation, home. Tex-Mexican, Jewish, and American, all on one bun. If Jay's was a throwback to the days of yore, a meal at Master Burger offered the opportunity to get a bead on the present, to ponder the future.

I would like to tell you that my burger odyssey ended there. By all rights, it should have. If I claim to be an eater in search of the underlying truths that inform our dietary habits, then my ultimate goal was already in hand. I had, over the course of visits to seven or eight burger stands, developed a working theory of Los Angeles. Here's a distillation: The burgers of LA reflect the makeup of a city of immigrants. Influenced by the design aesthetic of oversized roadside icons and kinetic automobile culture, they trend toward the baroque and project a microcosm of heterogeneous America.

But I couldn't leave well enough alone. I ate again. Before my week in the Valley was over, I would sample a Bouncer Burger from the Gutter (the aforementioned bowling alley grill), and revel in the transcendent combination of delicately fried sunny-side up egg and dill-horseradish mayonnaise they lavished on a hand-formed hamburger patty. I would eat twice at Chronis Famous Sandwich Shop, a Greek-owned East LA stand where the stellar chili has a sort of porridge-like consistency that proved, in the end, all-important to matters of structural integrity.

And I would belly up to the counter at Father's Office, a retro hang in Santa Monica where the bacon compote atop the burgers was lovely, and the sweet potato fries were *en pointe* (especially when dipped into a crock of blue cheese), but the service was haughty enough to make me want to draw the bartender across my knee and spank him for insubordination.

Upon returning home and thinking over that encounter, I've come to see it as yet another reason I should have stopped with my pastrami chili-cheese at Master Burger. If Master Burger is not LA, if a pastrami chili-cheeseburger is not baroque, then I don't know what is.

Born in East LA Burgers

The chiliburger has not been subject to the same sort of scrutiny as the cheeseburger. As far as I can tell, there are no ongoing squabbles over who first swamped a burger-topped bun with a ladle of chili—with or without beans. Greek restaurateurs in the Midwest have long spooned cinnamon-spiked and bean-riddled chili on hot dogs and burgers. So have the grill cooks of Texas, though they would forswear the cinnamon—and

*the beans. In Los Angeles, diner operators have long called
the dish a "chili size," as in a burger with a bun-sized ladle of
chili poured atop. And the older-generation cooks will tell you
that Tommy DeForest divined both the dish and the name.*

- 1 medium onion, chopped
- 1 tablespoon vegetable oil or olive oil
- 1 pound ground chuck
- 2 cloves fresh garlic, chopped
- 1 cup tomato sauce
- 1 cup water
- ½ teaspoon cinnamon
- 1 teaspoon salt
- 1 teaspoon cumin
- 1 heaping tablespoon chili powder
- 1 teaspoon paprika
- ¼ teaspoon cayenne pepper (or to taste)
- 1 teaspoon oregano
- 3 tablespoons cornmeal

In a large skillet, sauté the onions in the oil until they
soften. Add the meat and half of the garlic and cook
until the meat is no longer pink. Add the tomato sauce
and water. Heat to a boil, and then reduce to a simmer.
Now stir in the remaining half of the garlic, and the
cinnamon, salt, cumin, chili powder, paprika, cayenne,

(continued)

and oregano. Cook, uncovered, for 30 minutes, stirring occasionally to prevent sticking. After half an hour, sprinkle the cornmeal over the chili and stir to combine. Cook for 30 more minutes.

BURGERS
- 4 buns
- ½ cup chopped onion
- 4 slices American cheese
- Basic burger recipe (see page 174)
- Shredded lettuce or cabbage
- Thousand Island dressing

Toast 4 buns. Smear chili on bottom bun. Sprinkle chopped onion on bottom bun. Top with cheese-draped patty. Add shredded lettuce or cabbage. Spread Thousand Island dressing on top bun, put together, and serve. *Makes enough chili for 6 burgers, with leftovers. Note that the chili takes 1 hour to cook.*

Slouching Toward a Theory of the Fry

r andom facts: McDonald's cooks 7 percent of the potatoes harvested in the United States. The average length of a McDonald's fry is three inches. Laid end-to-end, McDonald's annual output of three-inchers would circle the equator nearly five hundred times. McDonald's holds fries in a warmer for a maximum of five minutes; unsold fries are tossed in recycling bins and shipped to the Kobuck Valley of Alaska, where entrepreneurs use them as insulation when building all manner of structures, including single-family homes. (That last part is a fiction.)

I'm not a fan of McDonald's burgers, which are better understood as fuel rather than food. But I dote on their fries. Sandpaper on the outside, cotton ball on the inside, they are golden splinters, arguable proof that better living—and better eating—may well be achievable through technology.

Fries were "almost sacrosanct for me," Ray Kroc wrote in his autobiography, their "preparation a ritual to be followed religiously. . . . Fries gave us an identity, an exclusiveness." (In 1960, Kroc told a newspaper reporter of another reason his restaurants were superior: "We don't allow jukeboxes, cigarette machines, or phone booths—and we don't hire female help.")

During the chain's early years, McDonald's employees peeled, cut, and cooked all of their own potatoes. As the chain expanded nationwide in the mid-1960s, it worked to standardize its fries. The company opened a de facto research lab, dedicated to transforming fry cookery from an art into a science. Among the outputs was a time- and temperature-monitored deep fryer, which signaled when a basket of fries reached its golden ideal. Another answer was par-cooked frozen fries, to which McDonald's converted all its locations by 1972.

That's about the year I first tasted McDonald's fries. I was ten years old. Until then, I didn't know what all the fuss was about. I remember the fries at the Bantam Chef in my Georgia hometown as limp. I recall the krinkle kuts from our cross-town ice-cream stand as greasy. But at McDonald's, twelve miles away at the base of an interstate off-ramp in the comparative metropolis of Macon, I awakened to the possibilities of oil-parched potatoes. The fries were cut thin, fried hard, salted liberally, and miraculously free of grease; I loved them from first bite.

They remained favorites for a good decade, until I graduated to Atlanta steakhouse fries, twice-cooked in lard; and poofy New Orleans soufflé potatoes, dipped in béarnaise. Even now, a sleeve of McDonald's fries remains a guilty pleasure. In a day when many chains dip their shoestrings in a starch mixture that promises supreme crispness but delivers an off-putting woolliness, McDonald's fries are my preferred off-ramp treat.

nd yet, my travels of the past few years lead me to believe that McDonald's reign may soon be over. In Philadelphia, reportage from which follows, I witness either the beginning of the end or a glimpse into the future.

We are, by most anyone's mark, one hundred–plus years into our love affair with burgers. To a certain extent, our traditions and tastes are fixed. (Most burgers I write about claim a history of four decades or more.) But fries are another matter altogether. They are relatively new, comparatively malleable.

The field of fry history has yet to reach maturity. Get a pack of dilettantes with good appetites and graduate degrees in the room and you'll soon have a dustup over dates and whys and wherefores. Conjecture is rampant, although it's pretty well accepted that we embraced fries later than burgers. By some measures, the conjoining of burgers and potatoes came in the late 1910s, after servicemen returned from World War I with a taste for Belgian and French frites. By others, fries came into vogue in the 1930s, when restaurateurs began buying efficient and relatively inexpensive deep fat cookers, or the 1940s, when wartime shortages of beef compelled cafés and diners to adopt deep-fried potatoes as an alternate/complement/supplement to burgers.

If burgers are modernity encapsulated, an entire meal

stuffed into a streamlined vessel and ready for portage, then fries are postmodern. Conceived as a side dish, fries now queer the deal; they command the center of the plate. Evidence is everywhere, from ragù-drenched shoestrings, stippled with mozzarella and bacon and dished at Greek diners, to cheeseburger fries, the battered beef and curd sticks now pimped at fern bars. Yet American appreciation of fries still lags. Even the classics of the postmodern genre have yet to get their due. I'm thinking, of course, about fry-stuffed burritos in San Diego, fry-girded steak sandwiches from Pittsburgh, fry-scattered pizzas found along the Jersey shore.

There was a time when burgers were new. And soon thereafter, we set about tinkering, refashioning, localizing. Now, when we play with our food, we're more likely to reach for a thatch of splintered potatoes. Mark my words: The fry is the foil, the tabula rasa foodstuff for the twenty-first-century palate.

the
future

FOURTEEN

Philadelphia Frydom

brendan, the bartender at Nodding Head in Philadelphia, speaks his mind. In a booming voice. When I order a basket of Spanish Fries, he warns me off. "Get the regulars," he says. "Our Yukon golds deserve to be eaten unadorned."

I do his bidding. And I order the microbrew he recommends. It's called Monkey Knife Fight, and it's flavored with lemongrass. By the time I survey the bobblehead dolls that line the walls—Evel Knievel, Richard Nixon, Beelzebub—my foam settles, and my fries arrive.

They are brown and rather stubby. The insides are cottony and the outsides are crisp, as is typical of fryers that cleave to the Belgian ethic of twice-cooking potatoes in deep oil, with the second dunk occurring at a higher temperature and resulting in a caramel exterior. But these fries are far from unadorned. In addition to being dusted in a salty spice mix of the type Emeril and his acolytes call essence, they come with a bullet of beige-colored sauce. My tongue tells me it's mayonnaise-based, and my bartender reveals that bourbon and pickled jalapeño juice are present.

I came to Philadelphia on a hunch: No other city in the country is as bonkers for fries. Based on my first stop, I think I'm on to something.

t he genesis of my hunch came a few years back when, en route to the Jersey shore, I stopped off in Philadelphia. It was late and I was hungry, and I somehow found my way down to South Street, playground of debutantes and drunks. One of the few places still open was the Copabanana, a Tex-Mex bar and restaurant, flocked in tropical wallpaper, that calls to mind Gauguin on a three-day tequila bender.

I ordered the Spanish fries. At the time, I didn't know Spain from Belgium, but I was curious. What I got was a basket of pencil-thin fries, heaped with blackened onion shreds and grease-singed slices of pickled jalapeño. On the side came a crock of doctored mayonnaise. I ate every last onion-entangled, peppery nubbin of potato in that basket. And then I ordered more.

I didn't think much about my discovery until I walked across the street and ran headlong into a stand called Ish-kabibbles. They sold Spanish fries, too. So did the Blarney Bar and Grill. And some hipper-than-thou place called Food Tek. All on a one-block stretch of South Street.

a couple of years passed. In the interim, I did a bit of homework. I flew down to Dania Beach, Florida, where Quebecois snowbirds scarf down poutine, a dish of fries topped with cheese curds and smothered in gravy. While there, I ate my weight in regular poutine, but refused tablemates who insisted I try their spaghetti sauce–drenched poutine Italienne.

I joined the parental rabble who condemned Ore-Ida's Cocoa Crispers, the new chocolate-dusted frozen fries. (But I secretly pined for the ones they market as Sour Cream and Jive.) I heard rumors of cheeseburger fries. According to press reports, these deep-fried sticks of extruded beef and processed cheese have been sweeping the nation since they were introduced to a clamorous public in early 2003. (I've yet to see them on a single menu.)

I traveled to New York and took a seat at Dim Sum Go Go, a swish place on the cusp of Chinatown, where a foursome of cilantro-spiked meat patties came tucked in dumpling-like buns with a sheath of taro fries. In Chicago, At Max's Italian Beef, I spooned fiery giardiniera on my cheese-gravy-onion-loaded ghetto fries and ordered a chicken Vesuvio sandwich for the road.

Out west, I lapped garlic fries. At Taylor's Refresher, a Napa Valley drive-in, I drank a glass of leggy Zinfandel and inhaled a thatch of shoestrings bathed in an emerald-colored sauce. And at Memphis Minnie's, near the corner of Haight and Ashbury in San Francisco, I shared a bowl of garlic fries and a bottle of sake with proprietor Bob Kantor. Over the course of an hour, we deconstructed the dish, arguing about whether smoked garlic or raw garlic or those little slivers of dried Chinese garlic play best off the potatoes.

Back home, I sidled up to the bar at Ajax on the Oxford square, and worked my way through an order of fat steak fries strewn with pulled pork and shredded cheddar. As I ate, I perused my notes and told anyone who would listen about the fry-stuffed sandwiches I had sampled at poor-boy shops in New Orleans and trucker hangs in Pittsburgh. I rhapsodized about the fritas of Miami, those nickel-thin, paprika-spiced burgers capped with potato sticks. I babbled on about the burritos of carne asada and pico-drenched fries I ate in San Diego. And I begged for firsthand accounts of the horseshoe sandwiches of Springfield, Illinois. Are they all that I have been led to believe? Is it true that one of the horseshoe variants is made by plopping a burger patty on a slice of Texas toast, pouring a basket of fries on top, and then drenching the whole damn thing in cheese sauce?

now the city of Philadelphia awaits. I have a half order of Nodding Head fries in my belly and a plan of attack that will take me to a dozen or so fry shops in four days. On the horizon I see bowls of the gravy-drenched fries that locals called wets. I see crab fries that have nothing to do with crustaceans and everything to do with a shake of Old Bay seasoning. I see mega fries, drenched in mozzarella and marinara. I see a need to stock up on Wet Naps.

But first I need a base, a meal of substance to see me through the greasy days ahead. At Tony Luke's, a South Philly joint set in the shadow of a highway overpass, I step to the window. Staring me in the face is a come-on for their beef-buster sandwich, loaded with house-roasted beef and a mess of curlicue fries. Yes, that's right; the fries are *in* the sandwich. And so it goes in Philly, land of the fry, home of the brave.

d ay two lives up to its promise. I eat the best Spanish fries of the trip at Ishkabibbles, and I talk potato genetics with Tom Peters, proprietor of both Nodding Head and another citadel of fries, Monk's Café. I eat hot fries at Johnny's on Delaware Avenue where, when I ask the grill man the secret, he gestures to a blond young thing and says, "They're hot because they were cooked by a hot girl."

But the highlight comes at a friend's birthday party, when I meet youngster Ben Robling. He's a staffer at Di Bruno's, the city's premier vendor of fine Italian cheeses. When I broach the subject of fries, I expect him to grab a wedge of Gorgonzola dolce and beat a hasty retreat. But he beguiles me with the story of a night he spent at his neighborhood diner, tucked into a corner booth, drinking a bootlegged bottle of Alsatian white, and digging into an aluminum pail of fries smothered in mozzarella and checkered with bacon. "Everything I've learned about how food and wine are supposed to work together was on that table," he says. "At that moment, you could have offered me a slab of foie gras and a glass of Sauternes and I would've turned you down flat."

I take heart in his words. They bolster my conviction that Philadelphia's love affair with deep-fried splinters of potato is somehow exceptional.

On day three I visit Di Bruno's, where I meet Anthony Screnci, one of Robling's coworkers. After he offers a taste of house-made mozzarella and I offer suitable praise, we move quickly to talk of fries. Like many a son of South Philly, Screnci waxes poetic on the subject. He talks of mega fries at Key Pizza. He talks of joints where they gob pizzas with fries and Cheez Whiz. And at the mere mention of the Crab Fries served at Chickie and Pete's, he breaks into a cheek-to-cheek grin.

Late that afternoon, I stop off at their South Philly location. It's a rather forbidding warehouse doing business as a sports bar. But Screnci knows his fries. These are thin-cut krinkles, fried hard and dusted with a cayenne-and-salt-enhanced analogue to Old Bay. And in keeping with what seems to be the abiding fry ethic hereabouts, they're served with cheese. All of which is to say, they're a near-perfect encapsulation of what a fry can be: texturally compelling, salty as hell, and—thanks to the Anglicized queso served alongside—teetering on the brink of pleasant vulgarity.

day four is a mess. A pall of clouds hangs over the city. And every few hours those clouds crack open and turn my umbrella inside out. I plot my plan of attack. But my heart (not to mention my stomach) isn't into it. My appetite is waning, and my mood turns philosophical. After a fruitless search for the perfect bowl of wets and a detour to the suburbs for a Fat Dutch sandwich, heaped with gyro meat, chicken fingers, mozzarella sticks, and fries, I walk down to the Copabanana on South Street.

Bill Curry, the man who opened the Copa back in 1978, the man who spread the greasy gospel of Spanish fries, is waiting for me. As I walk, I rehearse my questions. Could Philly's love affair with fries be a natural outgrowth of its parentage of the cheese steak? Could it be a skewed legacy of the Pennsylvania Dutch, who were keen on potatoes? Could it be a manifestation of still-simmering anger over the eighteenth-century decision to move our nation's seat of government to Washington, D.C.?

Over a basket of Spanish fries and a shaker of margaritas, Curry, a onetime newspaperman of good humor and great girth, embraces my notions about Philadelphians and their fries. But he's at a loss as to why. "Maybe it has something to do with all the Italians," Curry says vaguely. "They eat a lot of carbohydrates."

And then he lets slip a bombshell: "Everyone thinks I invented Spanish fries, but I learned them from a little Irish girl named Sarah. Hell of a cook. I think her last name was O'Keith. You know, she was from Tulsa."

My first impulse is to excuse myself from the table and book a flight for Oklahoma.

Spanish Fries à la Philly

This recipe was inspired by the culinary sleuthery of my friend Jeffrey Steingarten. In his book The Man Who Ate Everything, *he offers a recipe he calls Easy Frites, and attributes the technique to the great French chef Jöel Robuchon. With a bit of practice, I've managed to adapt Jeffrey's gleanings to the prevailing Philly fry ethic.*

- 2 pounds russet potatoes
- 2½ cups peanut oil
- 2 jalapeño peppers, seeded and sliced
- 1 onion sliced
- Salt to taste

Peel 2 pounds of russet potatoes and cut into ½-inch sticks. Rinse and then pat dry the potatoes. Pour 2½ cups of peanut oil into a 12-inch skillet. Add the potatoes to the cold oil, packing them in tight until the oil almost covers them.

Turn the heat to medium and fry until potatoes turn pale golden. As they cook, shake the pan to keep the potatoes from sticking. After 10 minutes, quit shaking and cook for another 8 to 10 minutes. Add a handful of jalapeño peppers. Wait 3 minutes and add a handful of sliced onions.

When the potatoes turn gold, increase the heat to medium-high and fry, constantly moving them around to ensure even browning. Drain and place on a wire rack. Sprinkle with salt and serve. *Serves 4*

CODA

Ruminations on
a Squealer

i t's early evening, first dark. I'm southbound out of Houston, Texas, headed for the hardscrabble warrens along Galveston Bay. The sun slips out of sight, and the flatlands unspool before me, void and foreboding. In the distance, an oil refinery, lit by a brace of sulfuric goosenecks, belches carbon. Pickups cannonball by, first blaring headlamps, then glowering taillights.

I sag in my seat, crank the stereo, spin the dial. I ate my first burger at eleven in the morning. It's now past seven. Three more burgers under my belt, and I'm still searching for a truth to glean, some sense to make of my binge.

I've eaten well. Robb Walsh—dean of the Texas food press, thinking man's omnivore—wouldn't let me down. He steered me to Christian's Totem, a backslidden convenience store

hard by the interstate, where the call of *gimme a cheeseburger*
sets in motion a chain of events resulting in a half-pound be-
hemoth, buckshot with jalapeño slices, draped with a neon
slice of American, served on a buttered and toasted bun,
tucked in a diaphanous paper sleeve.

Christian's burger succeeded by every aesthetic measure.
It was three-napkin juicy and loose in consistency, but still
managed to maintain, from first bite to last, architectural integrity. It was a classic, a textbook marriage of beef and bun.
But I want more. I have this notion that a truly great Texas
burger, a transcendent burger, should evoke Texas terroir or
persona. Maybe even both.

You could argue that Christian's fulfilled this charge. But
I wouldn't listen because I am southbound; the speedometer
is hovering in the high sixties; and Tookie's—the roadhouse
home of the squealer burger, the double squealer, the wine-
marinated French 79, and other assorted phantasms—looms
a half mile ahead.

i had entertained other final acts, other last-minute diver-
sions. There were Nutty Muffits—double cheeseburgers
with coleslaw and chopped mixed nuts—to be had at Bishop's
Fine Foods in Orville, Ohio. And I had not yet made it by
Bearden's, a roadhouse over in Cleveland that slathers peanut
butter on its burger buns; or the Wheel Inn of Sedalia, Mis-
souri, where the peanut butter goes straight on the patty.

There were fry rumors to confirm—of sugar-dusted shoestrings dipped in romesco sauce, as served in Boulder, Colorado; of datil, honey-drenched sweet potato frites, served in Key West, Florida; of horse fat–cooked waffle-cuts, served, on the sly, at a dude ranch somewhere south of Lubbock, Texas. But they would have to wait.

There had been a time, early in my research, when I had designs on digging through the stacks to uncover the truth about the $200,000-plus loan Howard Hughes supposedly made to Richard Nixon's brother Donald, a loan that was to secure the success of the long defunct Nixonburger chain. And I had promised myself that I would scour Iowa business directories to confirm that Lawrence Welk once owned a restaurant in Mason City, where the specialty was the squeeze-burger, served on a rhythm roll with piccolo pickles and—of course—fiddlestick fries. But that goal eluded me, too.

I planned to cook a Thanksgiving stuffing of shredded White Castle burgers, as developed by Kim Bartley of Columbus, Ohio, but time was not on my side. I failed to make the trek to the Younker's Tearoom in Des Moines, Iowa, where rarebit burgers come drenched in a cayenne-and-cheddar-enriched béchamel sauce. I missed my chance to eat a slopper at Coors Tavern in Pueblo, Colorado; or a garbage plate at Nick Tahou's in Rochester, New York. And I missed a couple dozen other concoctions besides. The ghetto burger at Ann's Snack Bar in Atlanta comes to mind. So does the soul burger at Ernestine and Hazel's in Memphis. I regret those omissions. And my stomach still rumbles to life at their mention.

------

b ut I do make it to Tookie's. Seated on a tree trunk bench at an oilcloth-clad table, in sight of a florid oil painting—said to be of the last private owner of the Hope diamond—I make my peace. Sure, I missed a lot. But on the road, in search of America by way of burgers, I did learn a few things.

In Oklahoma and Mississippi, I gained glimpses at the frugal roots of the burger phenomenon. And in the story of White Castle, I divined the liberation of the burger from a tainted reputation. In south-central Connecticut, land of steamed cheeseburgers, I learned that unheralded regional quirks still abound, that cultural homogenization is not a fait accompli. In Iowa, I came to appreciate the much-maligned burger chain—albeit a quirky one that calls to mind a loose confederation of squabbling second cousins instead of a cor-poration dedicated to burger throughput.

On the freeways of Los Angeles, I came to understand the burger as the apotheosis of a kinetic city of immigrants. On the Big Island of Hawaii, I discovered that my preconceived notions might be the biggest impediment to understanding what it means to eat local. On the streets of Philadelphia, citadel of the postmodern fry phenomenon, I foretold a fu-ture when potatoes claim their place in the pantheon of clas-sic American eats.

But as I sink my teeth into the cheese-capped squealer burger for which Tookie's is famous, my mind cycles back to the important stuff. I ponder whether grinding smoked pork into the chuck was a grill cook's attempt to construct the ultimate bacon cheeseburger or a drunken lark of the Tucker's Tavern sort. I sniff the tendrils of porky steam that spiral ceilingward from my burger and savor the slightly chewy texture. In the counterpunch of beef and bacon, I taste my idealization of Texas, of rough and tumble, of chuck wagon and cowboy.

I take stock of my successes and find solace in my failings. And I fix my eye on the horizon, secure in the knowledge that my fries will arrive momentarily.

Appendix

Prejudices

A burger is made with beef. As far as I'm concerned, there are no such things as salmon burgers or crab-cake burgers or shrimp burgers. If you choose to grind such species into pastes and pan-fry them in shallow oil, call them what they are—fritters or croquettes or savory beignets—but don't sully the name of the burger.

And by the way, don't talk to me about birds. Although I have fond memories of the burgers once dished by the Turkey King, a squat take-away shop in Midtown Atlanta, winged creatures do not hamburgers make. Ditto grains and vegetables. Vegetarians are welcome to read along and indulge in a bit of gustatory voyeurism. Just don't think you can convert me to your ways. Your children will grow old and gray trying to convince me that a charred portobello mushroom packs the savor of a hunk of seared cow flesh.

Ingredients

BEEF

You know those chub packs of ground beef, the cylindrical tubes of plastic-sheathed pulverized cow that groceries sell at bargain rates? Well, forget them. They contain all manner of less-than-desirable beef parts. Look instead for fresh-ground chuck or, better yet, ask your butcher to grind it to order. A ratio of 80 percent lean to 20 percent fat is the standard.

Of course, you can also make burgers from leaner sirloin, and I include a recipe for such burgers in the preceding chapters. But if you're looking for a beefier taste, cutting the fat is not the answer. Instead, get your hands on some dry-aged beef and ask your butcher to grind it.

Here's a basic burger recipe:

- 1 pound ground chuck
- 1 teaspoon salt
- 1 teaspoon pepper

Combine the ground chuck, salt, and pepper in a bowl. Form the mix into 4 patties. Heat a heavy skillet over medium-high heat. Place the patties in the skillet and cook each side for 3 to 4 minutes for medium-rare. *Serves 4*

BUN

If you can find a bakery that produces crusty rolls or buns that are substantial enough to hold up under the burden of juicy burgers with all the fixings, by all means give them your money. Reality, for many of us, is different. If you must rely on grocery store buns, I suggest that you modify them in two simple ways: cut down on the mass of fluffy white stuff by scooping a divot from inside the crown; and, by all means, toast the bun, preferably just before serving the burger.

CHEESE

American cheese is the standard. It melts readily and tastes both innocuous and pleasant. Exceptional of the recipes where I call for Cheez Whiz, where I note that the cheese acts as a binder, or I am otherwise specific, you may want to substitute a nice slice of American cheddar, perhaps a hunk of the good stuff from Grafton Village Cheese Company in Vermont.

Techniques

There are few absolutes in the making of burgers. Most recipe writers will tell you to handle ground beef gently, to form patties with a light touch, and they're right about that. But ignore claims that a charcoal grill or a white-hot cast iron skillet are the only acceptable cooking mediums. Use what you have and keep the heat at about medium-high.

An aside on size: Hamburger Harry of Daytona Beach, Florida, doesn't like fat burgers, those fern bar behemoths that require knife and fork. "When you can't get your mouth around it, something's wrong," he told me. "You should bite through a burger with ease. It shouldn't require unhinging your jaw." In his plaint I recognize my own prejudices; I, too, like my burgers on the shy side.

Garnishes

KETCHUP

I'm not a big fan of ketchup, which tastes too sweet to me. "The greatest fans of ketchup," said Joe Allen, who opened his American bar in Paris in 1972, "are people who have been to boarding school or jail or both." I'm not quite sure what he meant by that, but I think I know how Thomas Wolfe, author of the 1940 novel *You Can't Go Home Again,* felt about the truck drivers of Manhattan who "poured great gobs and gluts of thick tomato ketchup on their hamburgers." Of course, for some, ketchup is integral; more power to you.

MUSTARD

Order a burger, a regular ol' burger at the queerly named Health Camp, open since 1949 in Waco, Texas, and you get mustard. A little cajoling will get you some mayonnaise, though in my experience, you have to work for it. That seems to be the case with many old-style burger joints: mustard comes standard; everything else is embellishment. Although yellow mustard is the norm, I'm a brown mustard man.

EVERYTHING ELSE

Mayonnaise is a good lubricator of many a burger. Seek out the Duke's brand, which, thanks to a dash of cider vinegar, is tarter than the norm. Out west, a Thousand Island– or Russian dressing–derived sauce is de rigueur. And then there are the curious local phenomena, like the black-brown sauce that they ladle over onion-strewn patties at Milo's in Birmingham, Alabama. I'm a fool for the stuff, which tastes like garlicky A1.

Lettuce, Tomatoes, Onions, Pickles, and Other Products of the Garden

Onions, as I note in an early chapter, are harbingers of hamburgers past. Shave them thin, chop them coarse, mince them into a pulp; just use them. Pickles can overpower most any burger. I think they are best employed as bun-toppers, as hood ornaments. As for lettuce and tomato, have at it. But stick with iceberg for the lettuce; it stands up best to the heat of a burger patty. And restrict your use of tomatoes to the summer months, when they taste like something other than balsa wood.

A Note on French Fries

When it comes to eating out, great burgers are not predictive of great fries. And vice versa. In fact, the two are often mutually exclusive, in the manner of barbecue and catfish, which, as Southerners will tell you, rarely—if ever—are served beneath the same roof. Alas.

Great fries, like those time-honored Southern staples, require specialization. Before you heat your cauldron of peanut oil, you should know this much: buy starchy potatoes, rinse after you slice, always fry in clean oil, and drain on a wire rack.

An Odd Sauce for Good Measure

Smeared on a burger or served as a fry dip, this puree is pleasantly piquant. The formula comes from *Bull Cook and Authentic Historical Recipes and Practices* by George Leonard Herter and Berthe E. Herter, a contrarian's cookbook, which includes such practical asides as "Norwegian Method for Getting Rid of Rats" and such recipes as "Doves Wyatt Earp" and "Duck Genghis Khan."

Bull Cook Burger Sauce

- 1 cup sauerkraut
- 1 cup dill pickle slices
- 1 small onion, chopped
- 1 clove garlic, smashed
- 1 scant teaspoon Tabasco

Drain the sauerkraut and reserve the juice in a separate bowl. Puree all ingredients together in a blender, adding sauerkraut juice if necessary to get a smooth consistency. Serve at room temperature or store chilled.

Makes 2 cups (plenty for lots of burgers—would be great on hot dogs, too!)

Black Book of Burgers

NORTHEAST

DB Bistro Moderne
55 W. 44th St.
New York, New York
212-391-2400

Sara J's
7 Ward St.
Wallingford, Connecticut
203-294-0801

Shake Shack (open
    April–November)
Madison Square Park
New York, New York
212-889-6600

Ted's
1046 Broad St.
Meriden, Connecticut
203-237-6660

White Mana
358 River St.
Hackensack, New Jersey
201-342-0914

SOUTHEAST

Ajax Diner
118 Courthouse Sq.
Oxford, Mississippi
662-232-8880

Bean Barn
515 E. Church St.
Greeneville, Tennessee
423-638-8329

Bozo's
3117 21st St.
Metairie, Louisiana
504-831-8666

Bradley's
3695 Germantown Rd. Ext.
Memphis,
    Tennessee
901-368-4395

Dyer's Café
4774 Summer Ave.
Memphis, Tennessee
901-680-9887

Eddie's
1301 Assembly St.
Columbia, South Carolina
803-779-6222

El Mago de las Fritas
5828 S.W. 8th St.
Miami, Florida
305-266-8486

El Rey de las Fritas
1177 S.W. 8th St.
Miami, Florida
305-858-4223

Ferrell's Snappy Service
1001 S. Main St.
Hopkinsville, Kentucky
270-886-1445

Fincher's Barbecue
891 Gray Hwy.
Macon, Georgia
478-743-5866

Hamburger Harry
1000 N. Beach St.
Daytona Beach,
    Florida
386-254-8753

Jim 'N Nick's
220 Oxmoor Rd.
Birmingham, Alabama
205-945-0043

Lee's Hamburgers
904 Veterans Blvd.
Metairie, Louisiana
504-836-6804

Ollie's Trolley
978 S. 3rd St.
Louisville, Kentucky
502-347-6119

Ollie's Trolley
425 12th St. N.W.
Washington, D.C.
202-347-6119

Tucker's Tavern
635 N. Roman St.
New Orleans,
    Louisiana
504-522-0440

Varsity Drive-In
61 North Ave.
Atlanta, Georgia
404-881-1706

Weeks Café
100 Mill St.
Booneville, Mississippi
662-720-2151

MIDWEST

Band Box
728 S. 10th St.
Minneapolis, Minnesota
612-332-0850

Canteen
112 E. 2nd St.
Ottumwa, Iowa
641-682-5320

Cozy Inn
108 N. 7th St.
Salina, Kansas
785-825-2699

Johnnie's Grill
301 S. Rock Island Ave.
El Reno, Oklahoma
405-262-4721

King's Place
14460 240th St. (Hwy. 61)
Miesville, Minnesota
651-437-1418

Matt's Bar
3500 Cedar Ave. S.
Minneapolis,
    Minnesota
612-722-7072

Ollie's Trolley
1601 Central Ave.
Cincinnati, Ohio
513-381-6100

Sid's Diner
300 S. Choctaw Ave.
El Reno, Oklahoma
405-262-7757

Snook Inn
221 1st Ave. E.
Newton, Iowa
641-792-7303

Solly's Grille
429 N. Port
    Washington Rd.
Milwaukee, Wisconsin
414-332-8808

Tastee Inn and Out
2610 Gordon Dr.
Sioux City, Iowa
712-255-0857

Taylor's Maid-Rite
106 S. 3rd Ave.
Marshalltown, Iowa
641-753-9684

Vincent
1100 Nicollet Ave.
Minneapolis, Minnesota
612-630-1189

SOUTHWEST

Billy T's Burger Shoppe
1017 Austin Hwy.
San Antonio, Texas
210-828-0111

Bobcat Bite
Las Vegas Hwy.
Santa Fe, New Mexico
505-983-5319

Cappy's Restaurant
5011 Broadway St.
San Antonio, Texas
210-828-9669

Casbeer's
1719 Blanco Rd.
San Antonio, Texas
210-732-3511

Dave's Not Here
1155 Hickox
Santa Fe, New Mexico
505-983-7060

Horseman's Haven
4354 Cerillos Rd.
Santa Fe, New Mexico
505-471-5420

Owl Bar
Hwy. 380
San Antonio, New Mexico
505-835-9946

Tomasita's
500 S. Guadalupe St.
Santa Fe, New Mexico
505-983-5721

Tookie's
1202 Bayport Blvd.
Seabrook, Texas
281-474-3444

WEST

Café 100
969 Kilauea Ave.
Hilo, Hawaii
808-935-8683

Chronis Famous
   Sandwich Shop
5825 Whittier Blvd.
Los Angeles, California
323-728-7806

Diamondhead Market
   and Grill
3575 Campbell Ave.
Honolulu, Hawaii
808-732-0077

Father's Office
1018 Montana Ave.
Santa Monica,
   California
310-393-2337

The Gutter
Mr. T's Bowl
5621½ N. Figueroa Ave.
Los Angeles, California
323-256-4859

Jay's Jayburgers
4481 Santa Monica Blvd.
Los Angeles, California
323-666-5204

Koji's Bento Corner
52 Ponahawai St.
Hilo, Hawaii
808-935-1417

Master Burger
4419 Western Ave.
Los Angeles, California
323-295-1940

Memphis Minnie's
576 Haight St.
San Francisco, California
415-864-7675

Mike's Sandwich Shop
1717 S. Soto
Los Angeles, California
323-264-0444

Sam Choy's
580 N. Nimitz Hwy.
Honolulu, Hawaii
808-545-7979

Tom's #5
4497 W. Pico Blvd.
Los Angeles, California
323-937-2489

Black Book of Fries

Ajax Diner
118 Courthouse Sq.
Oxford, Mississippi
662-232-8880

Chickie and Pete's
1526 Packer Ave.
Philadelphia, Pennsylvania
215-218-0500

Copabanana
344 South St.
Philadelphia, Pennsylvania
215-238-1512

Dim Sum Go Go
5 E. Broadway
New York, New York
212-732-0796

Ishkabibble's Eatery
227 South St.
Philadelphia, Pennsylvania
215-923-4337

Key Food Pizza
1846 S. 12th St.
Philadelphia, Pennsylvania
215-551-7111

Max's Italian Beef
5754 N. Western Ave.
Chicago, Illinois
773-989-8200

Memphis Minnie's
576 Haight St.
San Francisco, California
415-864-7675

Monk's Café
264 S. 16th St.
Philadelphia, Pennsylvania
215-545-7005

Nodding Head
1516 Sansom St.
Philadelphia, Pennsylvania
215-569-9525

Taylor's Refresher
933 Main St.
St. Helena, California
707-963-3486

Tony Luke's
39 E. Oregon Ave.
Philadelphia, Pennsylvania
215-551-4725

Thanks

The supporting cast is large and ever-generous. My editor, Jennifer Hershey, assisted by Rich Florest, offered excellent counsel and a keen eye. Editor David Highfill picked up the baton in the months before publication. Thanks, David. My agent, David Black, proved both friend and advocate. Megan Millenky and Mih-Ho Cha at Putnam drummed up great press for books one and two. Amy Evans, my Oxford pal, shot another round of compelling photos. My friend Angie Mosier tested all the recipes and gently corrected my mistakes. My wife, Blair, and my son, Jess, submitted to an all burger-and-fries diet.

Lance Elko of *Attaché* gave me ink. So did Marika McElroy of *Travel+Life*. As I was putting this book to bed, the *Oxford American*—where one of the essays herein first appeared—

came to life again. Hurrah! Thanks to my colleagues there, Marc Smirnoff, Paul Reyes, and Carol Ann Fitzgerald.

A survey of burgers and fries requires the input of many a student of Americana. Jonathan Gold lit the way in Los Angeles with his book *Counter Intelligence*. David Hogan's *Selling 'em by the Sack: White Castle and the Creation of American Food* offered unparalleled insights into the square burger phenomenon. I also drew inspiration from Jeffrey Tennyson's *Hamburger Heaven,* Jane Murphy and Liz Yeh Sing's *The Great Big Burger Book,* and Elizabeth Rozin's *The Primal Cheeseburger.*

Laura Ehret introduced me to the Health Camp in Waco and to the cumin-scented joys of the Hamburger House in Dallas. John Fockler chimed in at the last minute with Cleveland tips. Rod Davis and Karen Haram of San Antonio knew beans. Becky Mercuri offered hamburger sandwich citations. So did Charles Perry. Dara Moskowitz proved that Minneapolis matters. The folks at Phillips of Oxford sated my off-road cravings. John Currence listened to me babble and cooked my vittles. Robb Walsh and family fed me Houston. Lari Robling and Ben Robling and Holly Moore and Rick Nichols and Matt Rowley shared fries—and tales of fries—in Philadelphia.

Marilyn Wilkerson offered dairy burger tips. Susan Choi and Pete Wells led the way about Manhattan. Oklahomans Scott Cherry and Josh Raynolds lured me to Tulsa. Leslie Kelly shuttled me about Memphis. Malcolm White and Bruce Browning told me tales of slugs past. Viviana Carballo mapped Miami. Walter Edgar of Columbia, South Carolina, stirred pimento cheese stories. Sara Roahen plotted my stay in Santa Fe. Bill and Cheryl Jamison fed me green chiles. Carrie Seidman and Dave Dewitt fed me enchiladas.

Jane Snow, Eddie Vidmar, and Coondog O'Karma fed me Akron, Ohio. Matt Konigsmark and Brett Anderson dished deep-fried New Orleans. Joan Namkoong of Honolulu showcased her Hawaii. Dore Minatodani of the Hawaiian Collection at the University of Hawaii at Manoa dug through her files. Barbara Kuck of Providence, Rhode Island, swung wide the doors of academia.

And, as ever, the Writer's Colony at Dairy Hollow offered a quiet haven; Mary Beth Lasseter, Elizabeth Sims, and my colleagues at the Southern Foodways Alliance granted me leave; and my friends at the Center for the Study of Southern Culture at the University of Mississippi led by way of example.

About the Author

John T. Edge writes frequently for *Gourmet* and *Saveur*. He is a longtime columnist for the *Oxford American*. He is a columnist for U.S. Air's in-flight magazine, *Attaché*. His work is featured in the last four editions of the *Best Food Writing* compilation. He was a 2004 finalist for the M.F.K. Fisher Distinguished Writing Award from the James Beard Foundation.

Edge has a number of books to his credit, including the James Beard Award–nominated cookbook *A Gracious Plenty: Recipes and Recollections from the American South* and *Southern Belly*, a mosaic-like portrait of Southern food told through profiles of people and places. He is general editor of the book series *Cornbread Nation: The Best of Southern Food Writing*, and foodways section editor for the forthcoming edition of the *Encyclopedia of Southern Culture*.

Edge holds a master's degree in Southern Studies from

the University of Mississippi and is director of the Southern Foodways Alliance, an affiliated institute of the Center for the Study of Southern Culture at the University of Mississippi, where he dedicates his time to studying, celebrating, promoting, and preserving the diverse food cultures of America.

Edge is one of the founders and principals of the Civil Rights Commemoration Initiative, which is working to install a Civil Rights Movement memorial at the University of Mississippi. In 2003, he was named "One of Twenty Southerners to Watch" by the *Financial Times* of London. The award recognizes "Southerners whose achievements will have a greater impact in the future, both on the national and international stage."

Edge lives in Oxford, Mississippi, with his son, Jess, and his wife, Blair Hobbs, a poet, teacher, and painter. His website is www.johntedge.com.